The Book of
KALE

THE
EASY-TO-GROW
SUPERFOOD

SHARON HANNA

The Book of KALE

THE EASY-TO-GROW SUPERFOOD

HARBOUR PUBLISHING CO. LTD.

For Carol

HARBOUR PUBLISHING CO. LTD.
P.O. Box 219, Madeira Park, BC, V0N 2H0
www.harbourpublishing.com

Photography by Christina Symons © 2012, except where noted
Edited by Carol Pope and Cliff Rowlands
Cover and text design by Five Seventeen/Picapica.ca
Printed and bound in Canada

Canada Council
for the Arts

Conseil des Arts
du Canada

BRITISH COLUMBIA
ARTS COUNCIL
An agency of the Province of British Columbia

Harbour Publishing acknowledges financial support from the
Government of Canada through the Canada Book Fund and
the Canada Council for the Arts, and from the Province of
British Columbia through the BC Arts Council and the Book
Publishing Tax Credit.

LIBRARY AND ARCHIVES CANADA CATALOGUING IN PUBLICATION

Hanna, Sharon
The book of kale : the easy-to-grow superfood / Sharon Hanna.

Includes index.
ISBN 978-1-55017-576-9

1. Kale.
2. Vegetable gardening.
3. Cooking (Greens).
4. Cookbooks. I. Title.

SB351.K3H36 2012   635'.347   c2012-900569-x

ADDITIONAL PHOTO CREDITS: Cover, upper left: *Chris Price/iStock*; back
cover author portrait: *Joe Lederer Photography*; p.4: 'Red Russian'
bouquet. *Diana Batts photo*; p.10: 'Red Russian'. *Wade Sisler photo*; p. 12:
'Redbor' and 'Red Russian'. *Mona Makela/iStock*; p.16: Tuscan (a.k.a.
dinosaur, 'Lacinato', palm) kale. *Graham Rice/GardenPhotos.com*; p. 19:
Wilson, Norman. *Your own vegetables all the year round—: if you dig
for victory now.* UNT Digital Library. http://digital.library.unt.edu/
ark:/67531/metadc540/. Accessed February 1, 2012; p. 22: Seedlings
in cold frames and 'Blue Curled Scots'. *Graham Rice/GardenPhotos.
com*; p. 26: 'Redbor' in a mixed flower and vegetable border. *judywhite/
GardenPhotos.com*; p. 42: *Richard Clark/istock*; p. 46: Kale microgreens.
Christina Symons photo; p. 50: 'Lacinato' as garden design element.
Graham Rice/GardenPhotos.com; p. 56: Organic curly kale for sale.
Dan Moore/iStock; p. 185: Tuscan kale. *Robert Sarno/iStock*.

Acknowledgements

To Carol Pope, my editor and midwife for this book in so many ways—thank you for knowing exactly what was needed, especially when I did not. I could not have done it without you! Thanks as well to her partner Cliff Rowlands.

To everyone at Harbour Publishing—thanks for taking on *The Book of Kale*. I'm especially grateful to the eagle eyes of copy editor Patricia Wolfe and proofreader Kathy Sinclair, as well as to ace book designer Five Seventeen, expert indexer Stephen Ullstrom and marketing whiz Annie Boyar. And to managing editor Anna Comfort O'Keeffe, mushroom hunter and fantastic cook—thanks for your enthusiasm, for having faith in me (and kale) and for the recipes. All of it is much appreciated.

To Christina Symons—thank you for your kindness, and the beautiful food and kale photographs. Your studio, home and garden look and feel like Eden to me.

Thanks to Judith O'Keeffe, Christina Symons' mom and Odessa Bromley for the loan of many of the lovely dishes and linens used in the photographs.

Thanks to Quinn Dombrowski, Vivian Evans, Carol Pope, Nick Saltmarsh, Derek Visser and everyone who generously shared their kale photographs.

To Dr. Dean Adam Kopsell, "King of Kale" of the academic world–thank you for reviewing my nutrition information and being so available to answer questions and assist with scientific matters.

To Dr. Joanne Curran-Celentano, thank you for your enthusiasm... "gotta love a kale-lover!"

Thanks also to Julia O'Loughlin, RHN, for your assistance with the manuscript.

Many thanks to my friends and neighbours who tasted the kale dishes, tested the recipes, suggested changes, let me include their recipes in the book and otherwise put up with my kale obsession: Karen Luke, Paul Faibish, Barbara "Put Kale in That" Coward, Heather Nielsen, Princess Diana Batts, Veronica Smith, Karen "Hot Beds" Hodgson, Gail Davidson, Karin Ward, Wendy "Stary Eyes" Macdonald, Marguerite Bradbury and Jackie Jordan.

A special kale bouquet to Odessa and David Bromley who patiently allowed me to mess up their kitchen while prepping for the photo shoot.

Thank you to Dr. Peter Stovell, master of vermicomposting, for kale-harvesting privileges.

Thanks, Frederick Munn of West Creek Farms, for caring about making beautiful soil for growing clean, healthy food. Also for generally being a mensch.

To the late Dr. Nancy Hall, kale lover, whose courageous spirit was present as I wrote this book.

To my family—Ted and Jesse, I love you.

And thank you, Roger, for always saying "bye for now" instead of "goodbye."

CONTENTS

Preface

Repeatedly singled out as a top superfood by nutrition experts, kale is antioxidant-rich and bursting with phytonutrients—quite simply, it's a dream food. In this day and age when the average person may feel too busy to exercise, relax or take the time to eat well, when families are struggling to create fast yet healthy meals within a budget, and everyone is looking for a way to boost their immunity, kale seems just too good to be true.

The question for me for some time has been this: "Why isn't *everybody* growing kale?"

As a new gardener years ago, I was astounded by how easily kale grows in any garden—even in locations and seasons too cool for many other edibles. In fact, if the weather gets nippy, kale actually benefits from a good frost, tasting sweeter. In hues of green, purple, red and black, it is gorgeous lined up like little palm trees or intermixed with ornamental plants in the front yard, on the balcony. . .anywhere, really. Not only is it vigorous, it's resilient, easily winning the prize in my garden as the most problem-free organic green ever grown.

Planting kale with my family got us outside, relaxing and working together. We learned how rewarding it is to pluck fresh food from our own patch twelve months of the year, dusting away snow to snap off kale leaves for immune-boosting winter soups. In spring we nibbled on tender buds from last year's plantings while sowing seeds for a new crop. We tossed blooms into salads, peeled stems for crisp snacks with dip, loaded leaves into sandwiches.

Still the kale kept coming. . .and we began to ask: what else could we do with this wonderfood?

Enter Sharon Hanna, who (I can testify from time spent in her cozy kitchen) is an amazing and intuitive cook with a knack for making simple garden-to-kitchen fare memorable, actually unforgettable. After months and months in her kitchen with bales of kale, she has emerged with a beautiful and versatile selection of recipes that allows any family to eat like kings all year long. Whether you grow your own—and you will likely wish to, thanks to the easy and earth-embracing instructions here—or you scoop some kale up from a nearby farmers' market or stand (also a fantastic way to support local food), you and your family will find more than eighty easy ways to prepare and love kale every single day of the year.

In these times of high-priced groceries and fast food, *The Book of Kale* provides a simple, down-to-earth and delectable approach to putting life-embracing meals on the table while tightening up the budget and honouring good health. A firm believer in how cooking and eating (and growing food) together can strengthen a family, Ms. Hanna—winner of the Vancouver Mayor's Environmental Achievement Award for her inspirational work with inner-city elementary students—has made *The Book of Kale* an exciting, empowering and delicious journey of discovery.

Introduction

It's been a real kale-o-rama around here. We (that is, me, friends and neighbours) have endured every imaginable play on words regarding kale, from "o-kale" instead of okay to "kale, kale, the gang's all here," and "it's blowing a kale" when the wind came up. At least five hundred people asked if I knew about kale chips, and would there be a recipe for them in the book?

On walks with Pocky (she's now a kale-eating dog) and my gardening pal Barb, I whined and worried about kale—varieties of kale, how many plants do you need for overwintering, and was there enough broth in that soup recipe? From endless hours staring at the computer screen I felt certain that age-related macular degeneration had set in, even though I'd eaten kale three times a day for months.

Cooking has been central to my life for a long time. This began when I was about eight, which made my mother happy since she was not super enthusiastic about dinnertime. She did love to bake pies or make fancy moulded salads with Jell-O in the shape of a fish. If my mom, born Gwendolyn Frances Iverson, had been more into cooking, I might not have become so kitchen-centred.

With a little practice I believe anyone can put delicious food on the table. I happen to feel that cooking is essential and people need to do it as part of being human. My house does not feel right if there are no dinner smells by 6 p.m. or so—garlic sautéing or chicken and rosemary wafting from the cast-iron pot in the oven.

I hope you enjoy the recipes in this book and get completely hooked on kale, and start growing it for yourself if you aren't already. Kale has come a long way from being (absurdly) a throw-away garnish at the side of our plates. It is one of the oldest and most nutrient-dense vegetables on earth, not to mention incredibly beautiful in the garden. Even in winter when everything else is half-dead, it looks good.

"Only the best is good enough for the child." This quote by Goethe sums up precisely how I feel about including children in our experience of growing food. Children benefit enormously from their connection to a garden. I believe it aids them in remaining authentic and heart-centred in the face of mind-numbing technology, keeping them in touch with the magical mystery tour that life is. So please garden with children—yours or those of others—if you possibly can. Instructions for cultivation have been written in (I hope) a user-friendly, unintimidating way, and should suit anyone, including all brand-new gardeners, big and small.

Sharon Hanna

Vancouver, 2012

Move Over, Ancient Grains

THIS ANCIENT GREEN IS A NUTRITIONAL POWERHOUSE!

The stuff of legends and reportedly offering sustenance since the age of dinosaurs, kale is one of the earth's most health-giving, nutrient-dense foods. While extremely low in calories, it is packed with vitamins, minerals and phytonutrients (plant-based compounds).

For the sake of our health, both Canada's Food Guide and the USDA's new food pyramid suggest making vegetables and fruit the biggest part of every meal, while reducing our consumption of animal proteins. Meanwhile, our beleaguered planet suffers the ill effects of meat production, thought to be a strong component of anthropogenic (human-caused) global warming. So, for both human and planetary well-being, vegetables are looking more and more like the way to go.[1]

Of *all* the vegetables (and foods) possible, kale receives a whopping 1,000 out of 1,000 in the Aggregate Nutrient Density Index scoring system—catapulting it into the superstar category. This means it is one of the healthiest vegetables on the planet. And that's very good news, because there are a lot of ways to add kale to your life.

Awarding kale absolutely top marks, the ANDI score (short for Aggregate Nutrient Density Index) was created by Dr. Joel Fuhrman, MD, who specializes in nutrition-based treatments for obesity and chronic disease. Fuhrman is Research Director of the Nutritional Research Project and the author of five books. Foods are scored based on the equation health value equals nutrients delivered per calorie consumed (H = N/C).

Let's take a look at some of the reasons behind kale's awesome status as a superfood.

Kale contains mega amounts of provitamin-A compounds such as beta-carotene, especially when steamed or cooked lightly. This vitamin is critical for low light and night vision, as well as affording protection against certain types of cancer. The body uses vitamin A to keep mucous membranes—your first line of defence against infections—moist and supple. Vitamin A also converts to enzymes that destroy invading bacteria.

Kale is also an excellent source of vitamin C. One (raw) serving contains 200 percent of the recommended daily allowance. This vitamin is critical for growth and repair of tissues, helps make collagen, heals wounds, maintains bones and teeth, and acts as an important antioxidant. While lightly steaming kale causes a small amount of vitamin C to be lost, it greatly increases the amounts of available vitamin A.

Kale is an outstandingly rich source of vitamin K—100 grams of kale provides 7 times the daily recommended requirement. This vitamin promotes bone health and limits neuronal damage in the brain; its role has been established in treatment of people suffering from Alzheimer's and other age-related dementias. [2]

Kale is an important source of calcium. Experts such as Dr. Annemarie Colbin, author of *The Whole-Food Guide to Strong Bones*, believe that kale, along with other calcium-rich greens, is a better protector of bone health than calcium from dairy sources. The reason for this is the synergistic effect

Kale is available in a rainbow of colours, with curly and flat leafed variations. Here, (front to back) Tuscan, 'WinterBor' and 'RedBor' are planted with rows of cabbage. *Graham Rice/GardenPhotos.com*

of iron, calcium and vitamins K and C, which when combined with protein allow calcium to be used by the body efficiently. Considering that more milk is consumed in North America than anywhere else in the world, yet this continent has the highest rates of osteoporosis, this may not be far-fetched.

RAW OR COOKED?

"While raw is sometime considered 'better,' when it comes to eating kale, heat actually helps. This is particularly true if you want to gain the health benefits of the carotenoids (phytonutrients) found in these nutritious leaves. Heat releases these pigments from the tight hold within the plant and allows them to be absorbed more efficiently after digestion. Having said that, some nutrients, like Vitamin C, are more available in fresh, raw kale! Mix it up to get the most from your garden treasure."

— Joanne Curran Celentano, PhD

Professor, Nutritional Sciences, University of New Hampshire

Eating kale that has been lightly steamed has strong cholesterol-lowering benefits. Steamed kale binds to bile acids in the digestive tract, thus they are prevented from being absorbed along with the fat and are eliminated. The liver is then required to replace those bile acids, drawing upon stores of cholesterol to do so. As a result, total cholesterol is lowered.[3]

Kale is a good source of copper, manganese, iron, potassium and phosphorus. Also of significance: kale is *low* in oxalates, unlike other healthy greens like spinach that are high in oxalic acid. This compound reduces the assimilation of calcium and magnesium in the body.

And kale is not just jam-packed with vitamins and minerals. The newest research involves the area of phytonutrients (from "phyto," meaning plant). While these nutrients occur in all plant-based foods, in kale they present themselves in particularly significant amounts:

KAEMPFEROL

· Prevents cancer by deactivating carcinogens
· Is associated with reduced risk of heart disease
· Possesses anti-inflammatory and antioxidant properties [4]

QUERCETIN

· Inhibits LDL cholesterol (the bad kind) to promote good cardiovascular health
· Is effective at reducing the growth of certain cancer cells, such as non-estrogen-dependent breast cancers, leukemia and carcinomas
· Possesses anti-inflammatory and anti-viral properties [5]

LUTEIN AND ZEAXANTHIN

· Is absorbed and selectively sent to retinal tissues in the eye where they become macular pigment
· Protects eyes from damaging UV light, helping to prevent age-related macular degeneration and cataracts [6]

A daily intake of 4 to 8 mg of lutein is recommended by USDA Dietary Guidelines; raw and cooked kale contains 26.5 and 23.7 mg per 1 cup (250 mL) respectively.[7]

BETA-CAROTENE

· Pro-vitamin A carotenoids support maintenance of healthy cell differentiation, normal reproductive performance and visual functions
· Functions as a free-radical scavenger
· Enhances the immune response
· Protects eye tissues
· May suppress cancer development [8]

SULFORAPHANE AND INDOLE-3-CARBINOL

· Found exclusively in kale and other *Brassica*-family vegetables
· Implicated in DNA repair within cells
· Effective at blocking the growth of cancer cells
· Possesses anti-bacterial/anti-viral properties [9]

CHLOROPHYLL

Associations of increased fruit and vegetable consumptions with the prevention of chronic diseases have led to new investigations into the roles of chlorophylls as valuable phytochemicals. A recent review by Ferruzzi and Blakeslee (2007) characterizes potential health benefits associated with dietary natural chlorophyll and chlorophyll derivatives.[10] Chlorophyll:

· May be associated with cancer prevention
· Binds to potential mutagens and carcinogens in foods and aids in their elimination from the body

Additionally, kale is considered to be one of the best anti-inflammatory foods around. In short, kale may just be the most outstanding and efficient vehicle for getting vitamins, minerals and umpteen protective factors into you and your family.

Raw kale contains substances called goitrogens that can inhibit absorption of iodine. This may have a negative effect on those with hypothyroidism. If you have diagnosed thyroid problems, check with your doctor about this, and stick to eating your kale cooked.[11]

If you are on blood-thinning medication, it is best to avoid kale, due to its high content of vitamin K, which plays a key role in blood clotting. Not all blood thinners are the same, so again, please ask your doctor.

CAROTENOIDS IN KALE – THE STUDY

"Among all the vegetables, kale ranks highest in its concentration of the xanthophyll carotenoids lutein and zeaxanthin, the yellow-orange pigments plants evolved to help protect their tissues against the harmful effects of excess solar radiation."[12]

This is the finding of Dr. Dean Kopsell, Associate Professor of Vegetable Crop Physiology, who has been researching the nutritional value of kale for over a decade. At his former university, Dr. Kopsell collaborated with Dr. Joanne Curran-Celentano, Associate Professor of Animal and Nutritional Sciences, on the Carotenoid Project with a grant from the USDA to study the role of carotenoids in human health.

At the University of New Hampshire, Kopsell and Curran-Celentano's project looked at how well humans take up lutein and deposit it in the macula lutea of their eyes. The macula lutea is the region of highest visual acuity in the eye. Lutein and zeaxanthin are like sunscreen for plant leaves. It is believed that these two carotenoids have the same protective properties on the human eye. When concentrated in the macula lutea they can absorb and disperse ultraviolet radiation to help protect against cataracts and macular degeneration. Curran-Celentano also verified that eating a variety of vegetables with high amounts of carotenoids, such as kale, *is more beneficial than taking the same carotenoids in a supplement form.*[13]

How Kale has Sustained Us Throughout History

Long ago, Egyptians wished their pharaohs eternal good health by lining their tombs with intricate gold and silver carvings of garlands of kale leaves. That ancient civilization was clearly aware of kale's status as a superfood.

One can only speculate: did Cleopatra serve Anthony a kale Caesar salad? Did they sail about on the Nile, accompanied by their small-headed, big-eared cats, piloted by slaves, some of whom manned the oars while others fanned the lovers with giant kale leaves? If Cleopatra had eaten more kale, might she have survived the bite of the asp? Certainly, the Egyptian queen would have been well advised to heed the ancient Turkish saying that roughly translates as: "Every leaf of kale you chew adds another stem to your tree of life."

Playfulness aside, kale has been growing on the planet for a very long time. It was cultivated in Ancient Egypt, though a slightly different variety more adapted to heat, like the Portuguese type. But it was kale nonetheless and considered a food staple.

Going back a stretch further—a long stretch—paleobotanists have speculated that a wild grass not unlike kale covered the earth millions, even billions, of years ago. Was kale the food of dinosaurs? Is it possible that a terrible blight or virus caused the equivalent of the Irish Potato Famine—the "Jurassic Kale Famine"? Fossilized leaf impressions discovered where dinosaurs once roamed bear a definite resemblance to the kale we eat to this very day.

Thus, kale gives new meaning to "ancient" green. We know that kale has been under cultivation for more than 6,000 years. Possibly the oldest signs of kale are surviving ceramics and other remnants of ancient containers that once held kale-like vegetables, now fossilized and dating back to 4,000 BC at Shensi province in China. These ancient peoples might have used ceramic crocks to make and store a version of Fermented Kale with Ginger and Miso (recipe on page 78), similar to kimchi, adding lots of hot peppers to sustain their families during freezing winters. Indeed, they may have made their own version of kale chips by using fishing nets, strung up on poles, for drying the leaves in the hot summer sun.

Throughout much of the ancient world, kale appears to have been the most widely eaten vegetable in existence. Wandering Celts evidently brought kale from Asia to Europe sometime around 600 BC and because of its easy growth habit, sturdiness and cold-tolerance, kale continued to flourish and provide nourishment throughout the European continent.

Curly kale. *Sharon Hanna photo*

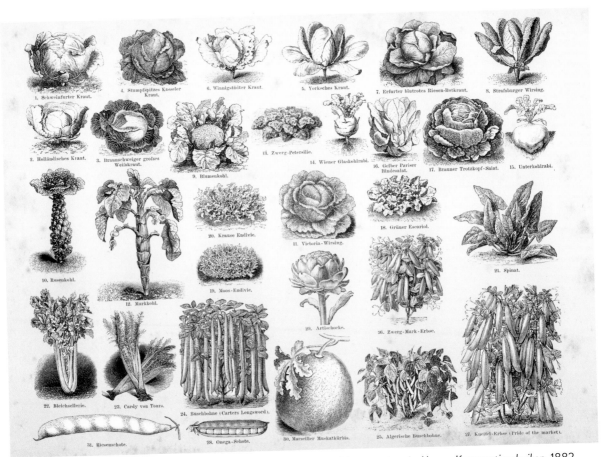

Markkhol, or Marrow Kale, is shown amongst other Brassicas and vegetable engravings in *Meyers Konversationslexikon*, 1882. *Ralf Hettler/iStock photo*

As with all good things, this came to an end. At some point during the Middle Ages (sometimes called the "Dark Ages") when medical knowledge stagnated, feudalism was "in" and war and turbulence featured on the menu, kale fell from grace. Possibly because the powerful had lost their heads (or would any day now), cabbages—perhaps the closest thing to kale *with heads*—eventually became the rage.

Kale's once-lofty status sunk to such a low that it was looked upon as fodder for cattle or other beasts, and referred to in denigrating terms like "cow cabbage." But thankfully, this was only for a brief blip in history. Lo and behold, along came the Renaissance and with it plant breeders in Italy who turned their botanical talents to creating new cultivars of the humble kale. "Tuscan" kale was born, more beautiful (they thought) than the common curly kale; stately *cavolo nero* was tall with elegant blackish-green leaves like long fingers—*Bellissima!*

Moving on up to the 1800s, kale came along with the Europeans to settle into North America. By that time, it had regained its rightful place in European food systems, and for good reason: kale germinated quickly and grew twice as fast as the cabbages with heads that typically took three or four months to mature. When you don't have a supermarket down the street, a dependable food source is not to be taken for granted, after all.

Reflecting its growing reputation as a wonder plant, all manner of legends and superstitions began to revolve around its sturdy stalks: kale was credited with mystical powers by many cultures. An old Irish tale features fairies riding kale stalks in the moonlight. When a farmer finds curly leaves thrown around in the morning light, it is a good omen and all his crops will grow plentifully, since they've been blessed by the "*kail* fairies."

A World War II poster from His Majesty's Stationary Office encourages households to grow vegetables (including kale!) as part of the home front effort. *UNT Digital Library*

In nineteenth-century Scotland, common language began to reflect the all-importance of kale: *Kail yard* meant kitchen garden, *kail* was used as a generic term for "dinner" and all kitchens featured a *kail-pot* for cooking. Meanwhile, *"have you had your kail yet?"* was a way of asking someone if they had eaten, or if they were hungry, and *"Cauld kail het again"* meant yesterday's leftovers served yet again. *"Cauld kail het again"* was also an everyday expression used to chide someone who kept telling the same fish story over and over.

During World War II, each and every household in Britain, Ireland and Scotland was encouraged to grow kale in the "Dig for Victory" campaign. Kale was easy to grow and provided important nutrients to supplement those missing from a diet depleted by food rationing.

From an ancient wonder to cow fodder and from food for hard times to the stuff of legends, kale seems to have played a part in history since the day of the dinosaur—and perhaps its sweetest role has been that of a messenger of love.

"Burning the reekie mehr" took place regularly in a place called Burghead, Scotland, at Halloween in the nineteenth century, when a kale stalk filled with tobacco was carried from house to house by young men who blew smoke (or tried to) into the front door. While the lads were puffing, the lassies were pulling leaves off kale in the tradition of "he loves me, he loves me not," to see who they'd be marrying.

As reported by one of the love-seeking lads: "I do not see the true Dwarf Curled Kale of my boyish days amongst all the varieties I have, nor yet that strong-growing tall Kale, which the lads and lasses used to steal blindfolded, to see what sort of husband or wife they were to have, and which was always enough for a good strong boy to carry on Hallowe'en night."

Leaf by leaf, the girl would call out the names of the eligible males. The name she spoke at the last leaf was her husband-to-be. Fortunately, the charm was reversible—if the young man was not to her liking, not eating the leaf would render the arrangement null and void. And, undoubtedly, no matter who the lassie eventually chose, her married life with him would be replete with growing, eating and enjoying the health benefits of kale!

KALE NAMES AROUND THE WORLD

China—*wou tu gai lan*

France—*chou cavalier, chou vert*

Germany—*blattkohl, kuhkohl*

Holland—*boerenkool*

Italy—*cavolo da foglia, cavolo riccio*

Portugal—*couve forrageira, couve galega*

South Africa—*boerkool*

Spain—*berza, col forrajera, col crespa*

United Kingdom—*fodder kale, cow cabbage*

Twenty Reasons to Love Growing Your Own Kale

1

You can grow high-quality organic greens for you and your family year round in most climate zones.

2

Veggies grown in good soil, especially using organic methods, are superior nutritionally to those grown using monoculture farming methods.

3

Vegetables retain maximum nutrients when eaten soon after harvest. The faster it goes from the garden to your mouth (or the mouths of your family) the better.

4

Kale is the easiest vegetable to grow organically.

5

Kale is a nutrient-dense powerhouse with the highest concentration of vitamins, minerals and phytonutrients of any vegetable.

6

You can eat your vitamins, minerals and micro-nutrients in their original form instead of a pill.

7

Kale tastes sweet and delicious after a freeze or two. Store-bought kale is usually not grown in cold climates, so if you live in a climate where your kale can be kissed by frost, you can totally take advantage of this. There is nothing like walking out to your garden in late January with a basket and filling it with gorgeous, healthy greens for your dinner.

8

There are more than eighty yummy ways to prepare kale in this book alone.

9

Save money on food! Organic kale, which is the best choice if you don't grow it, costs as much as a dollar per leaf. You can grow kale practically for free in the garden, in containers or even in a bag of soil on your porch. If you ate kale each day—simple with the recipes in this book—it would be easy to save hundreds of dollars a year on food, compared to buying greens at the grocer.

10

Lessen your carbon footprint by making fewer trips to the store in the car. Plus, no plastic wrapping or refrigeration is needed.

11

Gardening is a great form of mild exercise. Nibbling fresh kale from the garden while you are doing it makes it even healthier.

12

Gardening is great therapy—in my opinion, there's nothing more soothing or hopeful than putting your hands in the earth and tucking in some (kale) seedlings.

13

Gardening is a fun way to be with your family, and can be an exciting learning adventure for your children or grandchildren.

14

Kale is a very bee-supportive plant and other beneficial insects love its flowers too.

15

Kale makes great gifts—package up the seeds, make seed-paper cards, give it away as an edible bouquet.

16

Even if you don't have a garden, kale microgreens grow indoors easily.

17

In addition to being useful and tasty, kale is pretty—black, red, white, purple or glossy green, ruffled, curly, flat-leaved or fluffy, it can look gorgeous in pots, potager gardens or even as an edible hedge in your front yard.

18

Kale is self-seeding, so if you don't want to fuss at all, just put it where it can grow at will and you will always have it.

19

Kale is a super-easy way to make better use of some of your lawn space—just layer a lasagna garden over top of it and plant it up with this simple and pretty year-round edible.

20

Every bit of your garden-fresh kale plant is delicious—the stems, leaves, buds *and* the flowers.

Growing Your Own

Not only is kale an ancient superfood and deliciously versatile, as you have possibly already discovered by trying out some recipes—it's by far the easiest vegetable to grow. Requiring virtually no maintenance, super-hardy and quick to germinate, it is ideal for novice gardeners.

Like a weed, kale self-seeds readily; once planted and allowed to go to seed, most varieties will return year after year. It thrives in cold temperatures when other plants wither and die, providing a free source of organically grown, nutrient-dense greens right through the winter. You can grow kale in your garden, on a "lasagna" bed on top of your lawn, in perennial or annual borders, on your balcony in containers or pretty much anywhere there is soil and light.

And there are so many reasons to grow your own.

For starters, there is no healthier source than your own yard or balcony garden: just-harvested greens contain the highest possible level of nutrients. While store-bought kale is still a worthy addition to your family's diet, nothing beats fresh-picked from the garden for nutritional oomph.

Taste-wise, homegrown kale is also tops, particularly when left in the garden through a cold season—then it becomes incredibly sweet and tender. To survive a winter freeze, this innovative veggie calls to action "antifreeze" enzymes within its cells, which sweeten the harvest to the point that kids in my neighbourhood stop by (at my invitation) to snack on leaves and buds straight off the plants. Most if not all of the store-bought kale from supermarkets or specialty grocery stores is grown in agricultural areas that seldom (if ever) experience cold temperatures. Trust me—if you live where your kale can be "kissed" by winter frost, you will never look back after you grow your own just once.

Also, kale seed is available for dozens of different varieties that are gorgeous on the plate, as well as in the garden—and seldom seen in produce stores. And you'll save tons of money—even hundreds of dollars a year if you use kale as a daily green. So, why not bid *adieu* to kale that was picked a week ago, wrapped in plastic and carted thousands of miles—and get growing.

Your requirements are simply the usual suspects—sun, soil and water. Of these three, sun is the most vital.

SUN

The more sun veggie plants get, the bigger they will grow. Gardeners, especially those new to growing food, frequently underestimate the amount of sunlight needed. I believe that this is a major reason novice food gardeners might feel their thumbs are not green.

The truth: you can't grow food in a tree-filled yard that gets only bits of dappled light. Your kale will hang on for dear life because it is resilient, but won't produce much food. Since my commitment is to give you the best possible advice on growing kale (and other food), here is a cardinal principle: kale and most other veggies need a minimum of six hours of full sun. Those minimum six hours are best delivered in the middle of the day. The hottest, best-quality light occurs between the hours of

Veggies grown in good soil, especially using organic methods, are nutritionally superior. *Chris Price/iStock photo*

10 a.m. and 4 p.m. If your kale gets even more than six hours of sun, that's perfectly okay—it will be huge, thick and full, producing leaves like they are going out of style.

If you know right now that your yard doesn't have enough light, go to our section Containing Your Kale, on page 39, and grow a kale garden on your sunny balcony. Or convert part of a sun-drenched lawn area into a "lasagna" garden (see page 41). There are umpteen ways for you to enjoy growing your own organically homegrown greens, whatever your situation.

All this said, if you simply do not have a spot that enjoys six hours of sun, don't give up on growing kale. A solution that works well is to create a heat "island," simply a veggie bed situated against a garage or solid fence so that heat is trapped. This can act as a substitute for some of the full sun, and

was nicely illustrated by a good neighbour and gardening friend of mine a couple of years back. I was certain Suz wouldn't be able to grow food between her garage and a fence—but she proved me wrong. Manure from her daughter's pony made a difference too (well composted, of course—it's not a good idea to put fresh manure in your vegetable garden because of pathogens that might be present).

Suz's cabbages grew to the size of medicine balls and put my silly Savoys to shame. Her kale also outstripped my own—a little embarrassing! In this case, super nutrition and captured heat made up for a lack of sun hours. This is where you can experiment and see what happens. You have nothing to lose but the price of some seed.

And, lastly, kale *will* grow with a little less sun: with four hours it can limp along. Just plant more of it, as the plants won't grow as large.

Neither rain nor snow nor sleet nor hail watered *this* kale growing under the porch, yet it survived. *Sharon Hanna photo*

SOIL

Kale is a tough customer and can be grown with little or no effort whatsoever. Having said this, there are good reasons to give kale high-quality soil. Possibly the most important is that well-nourished soil produces more and better food. And, when tested, organically grown vegetables and fruit prove superior, nutritionally speaking.

"Good" soil can be achieved with the addition of composted organic matter. This is easily realized by applying your own compost or any other organic material regularly, about once or twice a year. Organic matter is something once alive and now dead or in the process of dying or decomposing, and includes (but is not limited to) well-rotted animal manure (from animals that are herbivores, like horses, cows and llamas), your own homemade compost or someone else's, hay, straw, leaves (shredded or not, dried or fresh), grass clippings, spent coffee and tea, newspaper and other types of paper, and prunings and seed-free weeds after garden cleanup.

At this point, it may be encouraging for you to know that like most plants (and living things) kale *wants* to grow—this is important, especially for novice gardeners. I have seen kale growing in the most unexpected places: the back of a gardener's pickup truck in just a smidgen of soil, underneath my low-lying back porch, in gravel and sand, and sprouting up from a crack in the pavement of my laneway.

Bottom line, the better your soil is, the better your kale will grow—but whatever your situation, it's worthwhile to make the best of it and get growing! You can also amend your soil occasionally with a modest amount of organic fertilizer made from such things as kelp, alfalfa meal, greensand, rock phosphate, worm castings, glacial rock dust and other naturally occurring garden boosters.

WATER

The last major requirement of kale and all other veggies is water. The only time for real concern is when seedlings are very young. Do not let them dry out, but at the same time, don't drown them. Overwatering is the number-one cause of problems, particularly for beginning gardeners (especially children) who think "more is better" when it comes to watering, even if seeds have not sprouted yet. More water will *not* make seeds germinate faster; in fact, seeds and seedlings require oxygen in the soil, so overwatering can mean death.

Throughout much of the year, rains take care of kale's water needs in most areas. You may need to supplement when transplanting, or during dry spells, or if you are growing kale in containers on covered balconies or other spots where they are situated out of the elements.

Sound like too much work? You might want to flip to the recipes in this book for inspiration on why you want to grow kale in the first place. Or, go straight to page 31 to read Cheating with Purchased Plants.

PLANTING

Please read the seed packages or catalogue recommendations regarding depth of sowing before you start. And avoid overcrowding seeds, as you'll only have to get down on your hands and knees later to thin them out—a waste of your time and patience.

Most seed packages and catalogues will advise you regarding two sowing times, usually spring and again in summer. Remember that you can plant kale seeds pretty much at any time and it will work out just fine one way or another.

PLANTING OUTDOORS

Direct-seeding kale seeds into the soil outside works very well. They germinate when conditions are perfect for their needs, and tend to grow strong and healthy.

SCATTER AND RUN

Laissez-faire types lean towards the scatter-and-run style of planting seeds. Farmers and experienced gardeners call this technique "broadcasting" and it provides surprisingly decent results.

Choose a sunny area in good soil (as described earlier) that is open and relatively clear of weeds. Scratch the soil surface only a little with a rake, and with a light hand toss the seeds around willy-nilly. This is how a mature kale plant sows its own seed—the pod ripens, cracks open and twists itself cleverly, sending seeds flying out to land where they may. After broadcasting, you can brush a rake lightly over the area to increase the seeds' contact with the soil and up the chances of germination. Either way, though, you will get results. This is a fun way to garden with kids.

DIRECT SOWING

Most gardeners prefer to plant their seeds with some decorum and choose this more restrained way of sowing their vegetable seeds outdoors.

You may direct-sow by planting three or four seeds in the same area, to be thinned out later (known as "sowing in drills"), or plant the seed in organized rows, where you drop a single seed every 2 to 3 inches (5–8 cm). These too will have to be thinned out. Ideally rows of kale should be at least 18 inches (45 cm) apart, but by planting more seed than you need you can favour the best and healthiest plants when thinning (and you can eat your thinnings).

As far as depth of sowing is concerned, try to plant seeds deep enough to keep them from drying out, but not so far down that they run out of energy trying to make it towards the light. The general rule of thumb is to plant a seed three times deeper than its size (so a .5-cm seed would be covered with 1.5 cm of soil).

After sowing your seed and covering it with soil, pat the area lightly with your hand. Next, water with care—kale seeds are small and you don't want

Kale "seed leaves" are double heart-shaped. *iStock photo*

to wash them away. If children are helping, this is an opportunity to teach them to be gentle with plants and seeds.

Use a fine spray rather than a blast from your garden hose. If the soil is already a little moist, you barely need to water. Dew and ambient moisture will be enough to germinate the seeds.

GERMINATION TIME

Kale seeds sprout quickly in warm weather, usually in about four to five days. In cooler conditions, the seed may take much longer—two weeks or more. Seeds often survive freezing, and if sown (or self-sown) in very cold months, kale won't germinate until the soil warms up a bit.

It's helpful to know what your veggie will look like when it sprouts, especially if you've never grown it before and are direct-sowing. Weed seeds are everywhere: each time you dig even a little or scratch the soil, more weed seeds are unearthed, and they will compete with your plants for space. It's good to know which plants are your crop and which ones are weeds.

Typical of the *Brassica* family, kale's "seed leaves"—first to appear and differently shaped from the next set of "true leaves"—are double heart-shaped.

Mildly flavoured baby kale greens are perfect for serving raw. *Carol Pope photo*

GROWING KALE AS "MESCLUN"

Kale can be grown as "mesclun," also known as the "cut-and-come-again" style of harvesting. Sown quite thickly at any time from March through early September in the ground or in containers, it is scissor-harvested, and the delicate, mildly flavoured greens are perfect for salads, stir-fries and sandwiches. Munching ("snackscaping") is also highly recommended while you're working in the garden.

Allow the kale to become about 4 inches (10 cm) tall; then, using a good pair of kitchen scissors, trim half or so of the seedlings off into a colander or basket. Avoid razing the young greens; be sure to leave 2 inches (5 cm) of the plants so that they have enough energy to regrow.

Half-strength organic liquid fertilizer, fish- or kelp-based, should be fed as a treat to your mesclun bed each time you harvest. You can expect to get about three or four harvests from each sowing. To provide a steady supply, sow for scissor-harvesting every 10 to 14 days. A 3-foot (1 m) square will give you lots.

WHEN KALE SELF-SEEDS

When kale propagates itself—also known as "volunteering"—a forest of very tightly spaced small plants tends to spring up around the mother plant.

You must thin them out when the plants are small (less than 2 in./5 cm). Otherwise, their natural instinct is to "bolt" (shoot up and try to set seed) as they are competing with each other—thank you, Charles Darwin.

HINTS AND TIPS

"X" marks the spot—it's a good idea to place a marker, label or an inverted empty seed package on a stick where you plant your kale seeds; note both the variety name and planting date. Fine-tipped permanent markers are great for this task.

'Red Russian' kale ready for transplant. *Carol Pope photo*

Gardeners typically ignore written advice—it takes away the sense of adventure. However, especially in early spring when there is a huge expanse of soil and your small seedlings seem lonely being so far apart, it is important to restrain from adding in something to fill up the empty space "just for a while." Remember that anything else you try to squeeze in will stop your original plants from achieving their mature size.

I sometimes use a different-looking soil—a handful of seed-starter mix, purchased potting soil or perlite—to cover the seeds in the row. That way I can see where the row is in case the marker gets knocked over by a marauding skunk.

GIVING YOUR KALE SPACE

Kale will need to be "thinned" in order to grow large and produce lots of leaves. Give it an eventual spacing of 18 to 24 inches (45–60 cm) for big, healthy plants.

This is an excellent reason not to sow too many seeds in the same place—so you don't have to spend time on your hands and knees squinting at the ground.

If you do have to pull some up, or cut them off with scissors, you can eat the small plants immediately in salads, stir-fries or soup—or at least put them in the compost, so absolutely nothing is wasted.

You can also tuck your extra kale plants into pots—quickly, gently and gingerly. Cover the seedlings well with soil and water them. Kale resents transplanting (the actual gardening terminology). This means it doesn't like to be moved once it has taken root in the soil permanently. But try it anyway. Share your extra kale plants with neighbours, gardening friends and complete strangers.

When you wish to transplant kale or any other plants, choose a cloudy or rainy day, or even do it at night—always avoid full sun.

STARTING KALE FOR OVERWINTERING

Having well-established, sturdy and bushy kale plants in your garden during fall, winter and early spring is a no-brainer—kale is *the* perfect food for eating in cold weather. With astonishing amounts of vitamin A and lots of vitamin C, kale provides terrific immune support during cold and flu season. And, as mentioned already, kale that has been kissed by frost is sweet, mellow and tender—far superior in taste to kale grown in warm weather. Given it's a snap, who wouldn't want a gold mine of organically grown supergreens at their fingertips during the time of year when fresh greens are less available and even more pricey at the store?

The period of June 1 to July 15 is the ideal planting window for most overwintering kale crops. Start the Tuscan variety of kale earlier—mid-May to mid-June, for best results. This variety seems to take longer to grow into sturdy and large plants shaped like palm trees, but it's worth the wait.

You'll want *at least* a dozen or more good-sized kale plants per person to get you through the winter. Maybe even fifteen per adult, a little less for young folks. That might seem like a lot but do remember that your kale plants will not produce new leaves from the end of October until mid-February. During this period, most plants go dormant. Kale doesn't die back, but it just sits there waiting for more sun; at this time, you'll be harvesting and eating most of the existing leaves. I encourage you to grow as much kale as you have room for, as it's lovely to have lots to share with neighbours and friends who you will want to turn into kale converts.

Either direct-sow or start transplants, following the usual methods described in this chapter. If direct-sowing, *plant a little deeper* in case the weather is very hot. Should you forget to water the newly seeded area, be on the safe side: you won't go wrong if you put ¼ inch (5 mm), or even a little more soil on top of the seeds at this time of the year.

Lastly, for your winter garden, be sure to take advantage of different kale varieties (see Seed Sources, page 192).

A dozen or so good-sized kale plants will provide greens for one person over the winter. *John Bloor/iStock photo*

IF YOUR KITCHEN GARDEN IS FULL

. . . which it may likely be in June and July, start your seeds for overwintering in pots as directed. As they grow, gradually "pot up" each kale seedling into individual pots. Situate pots of seedlings between rows or around the edges of your garden, where they'll thrive quite happily, being watered and cared for along with everything else.

Sometime in September or early October when summer squash, beans and tomatoes are harvested, transplant your kale into its new home. At this point it won't hurt for you to add a handful of good all-purpose organic fertilizer. Plant the kale seedlings a little deeper than they were growing in their pots, firm in and water well.

RAISING TRANSPLANTS

This is my go-to method for starting kale, since it's easy to control the growing conditions. As I have a fairly small city-sized lot, my vegetable garden has limited space and I must regulate the inhabitants somewhat.

Much-pilfered (by me) 'Red Russian' looking a bit haggard in December. *Sharon Hanna photo*

Kale is hardy enough that it can be started in small pots—a few seeds per pot—just about any time, but March to August is optimal.

> Avoid putting your own garden soil into the oven and heating it, hoping to "sterilize" it. The thousands of living organisms that our eyes cannot see in the soil will die and smell terrible. It will take a long time for the stench to leave your house.

Stick to store-bought seed-starter mix (unless you know how to make your own). In a little pot, sow a small number of seeds—six to eight at a maximum. You can fit a lot more in, but don't. Here's why:

· The seedlings can stay in their first pot for longer without having to be transplanted, so it's less work for you.
· Separating seedlings (known as "pricking out") is finicky, hard on your eyes, and time-consuming.

Less is more. Now, cover the kale seeds with a little soil, water lightly, and put in a safe place with lots of light, out of the way of cats and other critters.

If you want to get a head start in March or April, put your pots of kale seeds on top of something warm—heating cable, the fridge or another heat source. Seeds given bottom heat sprout quickly, so be sure to keep your eye on your seedlings and move the pot outside almost immediately after the seed germinates. Plants grown indoors for too long become "leggy" from lack of light and weak because it's too warm.

CHEATING WITH PURCHASED PLANTS

Of course it's not cheating—this is a very sensible way to go for busy people. Buying already-started plants (known as "starts") is the easiest way to begin your kale-growing adventure, especially if you're new to this. Garden centres, grocery stores and other vendors of plants in spring, summer and fall often carry an assortment of veggies. It's likely that you'll see varieties like 'Redbor' F1 (beautiful frilly purple/magenta), 'Winterbor' and other very curled varieties. As kale becomes more and more popular, there will be an increasing number of varieties on offer, so even if you have seeded lots of kale, you might like to try a few starts just to test other varieties.

Russian kale at −12! *Derek Visser photo*

'Red Russian' kale in spring. *Sharon Hanna photo*

YOUR KALE IN WINTER

If you get a large snowfall, it will cover your kale like a big white blanket. Do not despair—when the snow melts, the kale will probably look terrible, but as soon as light levels begin to return (around mid-February) it will begin to grow like crazy again. Remember this famous limerick:

> *There was a young lass from Vancouver*
> *Whose kale grew as big as the Louvre*
> *The snow knocked it low*
> *And down it did go. . . .*
> *But in spring it did nicely recouver!*

Around mid-February, the plants will begin to grow—slowly at first, but picking up speed during the month of March, and even more so in April. At any time, the raggedy discoloured leaves towards the bottom of the plants may be trimmed off and composted.

You can eat the new leaves as well as the kale buds for months and months, right into May or even June.

Bees love the flowers, so please do leave a plant or two full of blossoms for these wonderful and important pollinators. To learn more about plants that attract and nurture bees and other beneficial insects in your garden, see More Kale Adventures (page 47).

Did you know that a great many types of bees are ground-dwelling? Astonishingly, where I live in the Lower Mainland of British Columbia, 80 percent make their homes underground. This is a very good reason not to dig and disrupt your garden soil unless absolutely necessary.

Kale flowers, at some point, turn into seed pods, and then the kale sows itself at the perfect time in early summer—around June or July. If you plant it in September or October, it may or may not germinate, but at least some of the kale will come up just fine in spring because kale knows what it is doing!

HARVESTING KALE

Kale should be cut just before it goes into the kitchen for the best taste and the most retained nutrients. The usual method is "cut-and-come-again"—cut off the leaves that you need for whatever you are making but leave the plant to continue growing. Some gardeners prefer the "rip-and-tear" method. Hold the kale plant firmly in one hand, and snap the leaves off in a downward motion, again leaving the plant to continue growing. If children are going to assist you, make sure you help them hold the plant. When using these two methods, don't take more than a third of the plant in one go.

You can also selectively shorten kale plants; cutting shoots from the top of the plant will encourage growth lower down. This will in turn be covered by leaves—and so on. Kale normally acts as a

Kale blossoms attract beneficial insects. *Carol Pope photo*

Marvellous spring kale buds! *Carol Pope photo*

"biennial," a plant that matures during the second year, then goes to seed and dies. However, one of my 'Rainbow Tuscan' plants seems to have become a perennial. I've hacked it right back many times, leaving the roots in the ground, and it's about to return for a third go-round.

When the plants finally are allowed to mature (and you can hold this back from happening for a *long* time by keeping your plant well snipped), you will enjoy another kale benefit: the buds! Delicious and similar to "broccolini," they are fabulous with pancetta and lemon (page 136), in pasta, on pizza, in sandwiches, in crunchy salads. As long you keep snipping the buds and their tender stems, your generous plant will continue to provide this added bounty. At some point (gardeners differ here) you'll want to stop snipping and let your kale produce seeds, as it just seems time. Or you need to make room for another plant in the kale's spot.

SEED SAVING

When the seed pods look a bit dried up and turn beige, it's time to harvest and bring them indoors. It is best to do this before pelting rain, and since kale grows year round, you'll have to keep your eyes on the plants to see when to harvest the pods.

Often, when a kale plant has finally given its all, I will pull up the whole thing, knocking the soil from the roots, and hang it on the covered back porch. That way I have the seed pods handy to share with visiting friends.

It's important to keep the seeds dry. Eventually you can put them in envelopes or jars to store until planting time. Or toss the whole plant head-first into a large paper grocery bag and let the seeds fall to the bottom, to be scooped out later.

Also see More Kale Adventures (page 47) for other seedy ideas.

For no-fuss seed collection, place the kale plant upside down in a paper bag. After a few weeks in a dry place, the seeds will shake right off the stem into the bottom of the bag. *Carol Pope photo*

Save your own kale seeds and you'll have plenty to plant and share. *Carol Pope photo*

PESTS, DISEASES AND MARAUDING CREATURES

Compared to other vegetables, kale is relatively pest- and disease-free. A common problem with *Brassica*-family veggies is club root, where roots become swollen and misshapen. Kale is sometimes affected by club root in my garden (you don't notice it until you pull out the plant) but neither the production of leaves nor the growth cycle seem to be affected. There is really no "organic" cure for club root other than to stop growing the offending plant family for a long cycle (something I certainly have never wanted to do). Some gardeners use lime but I've never had success with this method.

APHIDS, A.K.A. GREENFLY

Aphids are a bugaboo everywhere in the garden. In my experience and that of other gardening friends, 'Red Russian' seems more likely to have aphid infestations than other varieties. If you do have aphids on your 'Red Russian', consider growing other varieties like 'Rainbow Tuscan', regular Tuscan, or the Scotch curly kales instead.

While most of us curse aphids and feel they should be eliminated from the planet, it's helpful to remember that they are food for something—most often another insect that, in the action of flying around, pollinates our fruit trees, veggies and flowers. Human beings seem to be the last to understand, in some cases, how Mother Nature works her mysteries. Ladybug larvae and adults and many other beneficial insects need aphids as a food source, but often it takes the predator (in this case, the ladybug or its larva) a couple of weeks to arrive and begin taking care of the prey (aphids). So if you are patient, the solution to your pest "problem" is very likely to arrive at your garden's doorstep.

Avoid overfeeding any plants in your garden with nitrogen (especially from "chemical" and non-organic sources); aphids are attracted to the puffed-up overfed new leaves and will flock to them like teenagers to the mall.

If you just can't stand to see the aphids on your plants, however, a good blast from a hose will wash them off. They have sucking mouth parts that are broken when they fall from the leaves; at this point the little critters are toast. They won't crawl back up and suck the plant's juices in this lifetime.

CABBAGE MOTH

This flitterer and flutterer is white, usually with a little grey spot or two. Not a butterfly (though young children often think it is), the cabbage moth lays eggs on plants of the cabbage family, usually from late spring into summer. Its accompanying pesky green larva, cleverly camouflaged in every possible shade of green—and matching exactly whatever cabbage-family leaf they want to eat—can bother kale, but in my garden this only happens with younger plants or seedlings. Leaves of older plants, particularly very curly kale, are usually too thick for the little duffers to chew and swallow. This is by no means casting aspersions on curly kale and the tenderness of its leaves. Occasionally, people report infestations, but if that happens, pick all the infested leaves, removing the worms, then wash your leaves well and freeze for soup stock—your kale will grow back.

Keep a close watch out for these creatures—you can't miss the damage, as they practically chew the leaf off, but in an obvious angular pattern. Turn the leaf over and there you are likely to find a satiated green worm if you examine it closely. As it really is *almost* perfectly camouflaged, you may have to look twice.

"Manual removal" is the suggested method of handling. What you do with the worm after removal is up to you—ducks and chickens would love to snack on them. One way to throw the cabbage moth for a loop is to interplant flowers like alyssum or other strongly scented choices to distract and mildly confuse the moth in its search for a "cabbagey" smell. Interplanting garlic could also be useful. Avoid monoculture, the planting of only one thing—biodiversity is the key to any healthy garden.

Want to keep chickens? Kale is a fantastic forage crop—chickens love it!

MEOW, WOOF. . . AND BAMBI

Speaking of critters, certain. . . shall we say "lavatory-seeking" cats seem to feel that by planting a garden, you have created a lovely, loose and weed-free area of soil purely for their enjoyment and convenience. A good way to keep them out of newly seeded areas is to criss-cross thorny rose prunings atop the area. Ouch! Animals will stay out, including the odd curious skunk or naughty raccoon. If you don't have roses, someone in your neighbourhood probably does.

Another effective technique to keep animals from digging in recently planted areas: cover the area with upside down black plastic plant trays, which potted plants arrive in from the growers during the spring or fall busy seasons, and are usually available at your local garden centre. Nursery staff are usually glad to supply you with as many as you can carry, as they receive thousands every year. This method works with seeds, bulbs or small transplanted seedlings. Light and water can get through the criss-crossed plastic mesh, and seeds germinate just fine. Depending on the pest, it may be useful to place a couple of good-sized rocks on each tray to keep them from being overturned. Remove the trays once plants have taken hold and grown sturdy enough to withstand the neighbour's cat (or yours) or the odd curious squirrel.

Even deer don't seem to be able to decimate the stalwart and trusty kale. Here's a photo of kale plants nibbled to the quick by deer who got past the "deer-proof" fencing—in no time at all, every kale plant resprouted nicely.

GOT SQUIRRELS?

Squirrels don't usually show an interest in kale but never say never, as they can be real pests especially if you are feeding birds and there is seed flung around. These little squirmers can be a real pain for gardeners. Squirrels regularly dig up my tulips when they are almost blooming and chomp on them, even sometimes unearthing the whole plant. They'll also go for bulbs, and sometimes seeds too, even small seedlings or plants, depending on how hungry they are, I suppose.

Evidently, coyote urine sprinkled around the area works well but is difficult to collect. So, to outwit

Bambi and friends ate every leaf off this kale, but no harm done. *Carol Pope photo*

With just a little care, kale will do well in containers. *Christina Symons photo*

these canny creatures, try strewing the area with human hair. Squirrels seem to be repelled successfully by it—and who could blame them? I asked at a local beauty salon and they were happy to give me what was swept off the floor after a day. The hair was scattered around the area, and the squirrels left my tulips alone after that.

CONTAINING YOUR KALE

Great ways to grow kale include pots, containers, buckets, recycled plastic salad containers, old rubber boots, discarded sinks or bathtubs. I know people who even grow food in an old hot tub, having made the decision to grow more food instead of sitting in hot water out on their deck.

When growing kale or any other veggie or plant in a container, it's useful to know a little about how the needs of plants grown in pots differ from those of garden-grown plants.

Plants grown in the garden are able to get what they need, sending their roots out to gather nourishment from the surrounding soil. You may have noticed this in fall when you pull up a tomato or other plant and see how far the plant's roots have travelled—perhaps much farther laterally than you would have expected. Those roots sought a bit of a certain rock, a dead insect, or some trace element in the soil that they needed to thrive. Plants are smart that way.

Since by containing a plant you are in effect holding it prisoner, you become responsible for all its needs, including water, sun and nourishment. This is easily done, as long as you know how it works.

Start with fairly rich soil containing lots of organic material. You can buy good-quality "organic" manmade soils, so it's just a matter of finding them. Many nurseries now carry bags of soil formulated for vegetables—just ask.

Food should consist of some kind of organic liquid feed, often kelp- or fish-based, or a granular food that you scratch lightly into the surface of the container's soil.

Water releases the food into the soil for the plant to take up—so, containers will need to be watered regularly, especially in warm weather and when plants are growing very quickly as we head towards the solstice in June. Many gardeners add quarter-strength fertilizer to their watering can and give their contained plants a feed each time they are watered.

FEATURING KALE IN YOUR DECOR

Try either a grouping of pots with a few kale plants in each, or have your pots marching up the steps on either side—an army of kale standing at attention for your visitors! Kale combines well with pansies, ornamental grasses including decorative wheat, rye and other "cereal" grains, chrysanthemums, mini sunflowers like 'Music Box'—really, kale looks great with a whole lot of plants.

Though beauty is in the eye of the beholder, some kale varieties seem more attractive grown ornamentally than others. I really like the super-curly 'Winterbor' types—beautifully blue-green in colour with a silver sheen, the leaves sparkle in light frost.

I'd happily grow this variety in a container on my front steps—if they had sun, but they don't. 'Redbor' F1 is most commonly touted as an attractive edible ornamental, but regular or 'Rainbow Tuscan' would make a big statement at the entrance of your home.

If you want to use large and/or deep pots, remember there's no need to fill them with precious (and sometimes pricey) soil. If you have them, pack leaves, dry or fresh, into your containers to the halfway mark. Neighbours will be happy to oblige if for some reason you don't have leaves at your disposal. You can also use broken-up Styrofoam, balled-up newspaper, empty egg cartons, toilet-paper rolls, or just about anything else to fill the pot. A garden-designer friend puts smaller plastic pots upside down inside large pots—it really saves on soil volume, and most plants don't need much more than 8 inches (20 cm) of soil to thrive.

You might want to start your kale seed in smaller pots or clamshell containers with holes punched in the bottom for drainage, in peat pots or little newspaper pots. Just don't start too many! Remember they will almost all germinate and grow, and a

Tuscan kale seedlings thrive in a mini-greenhouse made from a repurposed plastic clamshell. *Diana Batts photo*

large container of about 20 inches (50 cm) across could hold five plants maximum, if you want them to attain a good size.

OTHER WAYS TO GROW KALE
RECYCLED PLASTIC SALAD CONTAINERS

I use the very large two-pound salad boxes often left outside the back door of a local Japanese restaurant in my neighbourhood. While not particularly attractive, they are completely useful for growing "cut-and-come-again" greens, semi-mature plants, seedling starts or microgreens. They come with a handy-dandy top that speeds germination. You can also use smaller plastic containers, of which a plethora may be found in every store, stuffed full of salad mixes.

KALE IN A BAG

If you are unconcerned about winning a prize for elegance when it comes to trying your hand here, and lack garden space in sun, try "kale in a bag."

Take a bag of rich potting soil suitable for growing food, and place it in a sunny spot. Lay the bag out flat, poke a number of holes for drainage, then flip the bag over. Now, cut a few "X" shapes in the bag, staggered 6 inches (15 cm) apart, fold the corners under, and sow two or three seeds in each opening.

Alternatively, you can cut most of the top of the bag off, leaving the sides to contain the soil, then sow your seeds. Follow the directions outlined already for fertilizing, watering, growing and so on.

UGLY (BUT UTILITARIAN) BLACK PLASTIC POTS

These are what are known in the nursery trade as a #1, #3, #5, etc. (1-, 3-, 5-gallon pots—though the measurement is not accurate). A good size is about 12 inches (30 cm) in diameter, and about 10 inches (25 cm) high. You can probably grow three kale plants to a decent size in one of these, as long as you keep up with feeding.

If you want to make the pots look less ugly, consider lining them up in rows, then draping them loosely with burlap; coffee stores that roast their own have sacks available, sometimes for free. Or cover the pots with old cut-up bamboo-stick blinds—you get the idea.

LASAGNA KALE GARDEN

Yes, there's an excellent recipe for lasagna in the book, but this is a different kind! *Lasagna* means "layer" in Italian—farmers and gardeners have been sheet-composting for hundreds of years, which simply means layering organic materials to make a built-up garden bed without an edge.

Got a strip of outdoors somewhere that is perfect for kale? A small kale lasagna patch may be the perfect answer for you. If the site you have in mind is grassed, don't worry—just layer your lasagna garden right on top.

YOU'LL NEED:

Green Material (nitrogen source—a.k.a. "The Filling")
- Fresh leaves (ideally run over with your lawnmower or shred with a weed whacker—simply toss the leaves into a plastic garbage container until it's about half full, then chop them up)
- Green grass clippings
- Unfinished compost
- Animal manure of any kind (please know the source)
- Spent coffee grounds including filters
- Tea bags or loose tea

Brown Material (carbon source—a.k.a. "The Lasagna Noodles")
- Dry leaves
- Dry straw or hay
- Dry evergreen needles
- Brown corrugated cardboard or newspaper
- Any biodegradable paper in bits, including toilet-paper rolls, egg cartons

Plus
- Some good garden soil (your own, or purchased)
- A watering can full of water, or a hose nearby
- A few handfuls of granular organic fertilizer

On a calm day (you'll see why if you try this in high winds), lay out pieces of cardboard or sheets of newspaper in your desired shape on top of a grassy area.

If using newspaper, it helps to sprinkle the pages with water to keep the everything in line and tidy. Lay newspaper down at least 6 sheets thick (or position the cardboard), then start building your layers, alternating green and brown (filling and noodles, filling and noodles. . .). If you have fresh manure, let that be one of the bottom-most layers. Continue to build your lasagna, patting down well and watering each layer. As you get closer to about 7 inches (18 cm) of organic material, sprinkle handfuls of fertilizer (think of it as the grated parmesan cheese).

Now, add topsoil—you want a layer of at least 5 inches (12.5 cm) when patted down, but 6 inches (15 cm) is even better. The topsoil is like the béchamel sauce, or mozzarella cheese layer.

I teach this method of gardening at workshops and seminars, and invariably someone wants to know if it's okay to add "edges"—bricks or wood, or some other method of containing the lasagna garden. The answer is no, please do not add edges. For some reason, in my experience, edged lasagna gardens do not yield good results—in fact, they produce stunted plants.

You can plant your kale seeds immediately, just as you would in your garden or in a pot. Expect them to grow very lush (and quickly)—the heat generated by the lasagna layers decomposing helps them along, and they will be very well fed, especially the first season. If you are thinking of using the lasagna method for other crops too, a word of advice: don't plant root crops like beets, carrots and potatoes the first year. The top layer of soil is not thick enough to give them the depth they need, and the bottom layers will still be decomposing; by year two it should be okay to tuck in a few turnips.

Kids & Kale

Children in the neighbourhood regularly visit my garden, and delight in being able to pluck the kale buds and flowers (they *love* to eat flowers). Maria Rodale, gardening guru and descendent of the famous organic-gardening family, calls this idea "snackscaping"—planting things that children of all ages (and adults) can munch on while working in the garden, or just "beeing" with the bees and other critters as they fly to and fro.

In my garden, children have also asked (unprompted) if it would be okay for them to pick some of the kale leaves, buds and flowers to bring home and share with their families. Given the chance, kids can see kale as a fun food: when not munching it in the garden, they can chow down on kale "chips" or stuff kale into wraps, sandwiches or hamburgers or whatever, if there's a handy bag of washed leaves in the fridge.

Kale is an ideal crop for kids to grow. It produces a result quickly—within weeks of sowing, little leaves are available for nibbling. But gardening with children is so much more than sowing seeds, watering and waiting. When I ran a garden program at Queen Alexandra School in Vancouver, BC, students demonstrated that gardening-related activities contributed to learning in many ways including joy-filled moments of discovery.

> "Ladybugs are clunky fliers, a bit like Dumbo. If you want to help them, plant lots of flowers with large 'landing pads' like sunflowers."—Brian Campbell, Beekeeper and Certified Beemaster

GOOD FOR THE BRAIN

Grow all kinds of different kales with kids at home and school—if your child's school doesn't have a garden, kale is a perfect place to start.

Label the plants so they can get to know the names, and help them learn the Latin (botanical) term for kale and other plants—many children are surprisingly interested in this aspect of gardening, as it helps the world of words become more available to them. Perhaps most importantly, this activity makes them happy and proud to share new information with their friends and families.

For example, children can learn that kale is called *Brassica oleracea acephala*. *Oleracea* means "vegetable- or herb-like," and is used in botanical Latin for edible or cultivated plants. *Acephala* means "without a head"—guaranteed to get a few snickers.

At Queen Alexandra School, kindergarten children as young as five years were completely absorbed in learning and spelling the Latin name for amaryllis—*Hippeastrum*—writing it on the board with different coloured chalk. The Latin lesson was a perfect adjunct to our annual amaryllis planting activity.

KIDS AS "BUDDING" PLANT BREEDERS

Kids (adults too) can grow all kinds of varieties of kale together. Because of something called *genetic drift* (when things interbreed or mutate by chance), this will result in slightly different forms of kale coming up in the next generation. Some will be more frilly, more (or less) curly, shorter, taller, or slightly differently coloured—sometimes almost completely white.

Be careful not to overwater. . . *Carol Pope photo*

Eggshell halves are just the right size for hatching seedlings. Before transplanting, carefully squeeze the shell to crack it so the roots can get out. *Diana Batts photo*

Encourage kids to name the new varieties (botanists call these "cultivars") after themselves, their pets, or whatever they choose. When their new varieties mature, help them collect and label the seeds. A package of child-grown and -bred seeds will delight grandparents, relatives and friends. This could be turned into a great fundraising program for garden-related projects at a school—seed bred and named by the students, to sell to other students, teachers, and so on.

LEARNING, CARING AND STEWARDSHIP

Children can be reminded to let their kale plants flower at some point—not just for their snacking, but to provide nectar for the bees to fuel their flight. Children can also collect seed so they can plant more and share with others.

MOTOR AND WRITING SKILLS

Planting seeds is a great way for children to hone their fine motor skills—tiny fingers have fun with seeds. Writing labels for veggies and inserting them into pots or into the ground is part of the process.

Children love to dig in the soil with a shovel, and move soil or other organic materials from one place to another. Sometimes at Queen Alexandra we'd have one group of kids work together to fill a wheelbarrow with soil or compost and help each other get the wheelbarrow (no small task) to a destination in the garden.

Dumping the soil was next. Often the next class of kids would re-shovel the soil back into the wheelbarrow and wrestle it back to the pile. This was particularly relevant to team-building, and children learned about working cooperatively. In any case, we found that exercising the large muscles facilitated a much calmer state and excellent mood for when students went back to "inside" learning.

ANCIENT HISTORY

Plant a dinosaur garden with your family or at your school's garden. Include lots of different types of kale. See if you can locate the 'Walking Stick' variety—the seeds are a little hard to find but they are out there somewhere! When this type of kale is

Kale is the ideal crop for kids—easy to grow and easy to eat. *Carol Pope photo*

finished growing, you can use the dried stem as a walking stick.

NUTRITION
Kale is an ideal starting point for discussions around your child's knowledge of vitamins, minerals and phytonutrients, and what functions these perform in the human body. See This Ancient Green is a Nutritional Powerhouse! (page 13).

EAT, COOK, LOVE IT
Eat from the garden, enjoy kale buds with dip, make Kale Chips and Teen Apple Kale Toss (see pages 72 and 102)—all delicious activities to combine with nutritional science at any grade level.

We often used the staffroom to make soup. Students cut up the ingredients (mostly from the garden), then took turns stirring the pot. Eating the finished product and sharing it with staff and volunteers was great fun.

Of course, kids like to cook at home too, especially when they've been responsible for growing part of what's on the menu.

SHARING TIMES
Make homemade paper impregnated with kale seeds—put them in Christmas cards, make tree decorations, or give kale "hearts" for Valentine's Day (which can be planted right away).

LEARNING ABOUT PLANTING TECHNIQUES
Make your own kale seed "tape" with newspaper using flour/water paste.

Learn about recycling too! Washed eggshell halves, nestled inside egg cartons, can be used to grow kale seedlings.

THE AMAZING WORLD OF BOTANY
Learn about roots that anchor your kale plant so it won't fall over. Roots take in water, food, vitamins and minerals. Children can talk about what happens if *they* don't have enough water, food, vitamins and minerals.

More Kale Adventures

KALE MICROGREENS

"Microgreens" refers to a method of raising edible plants that are larger than sprouts but not as big as regular leafy salad greens. Unlike sprouts, they are not grown in jars, but in a shallow layer of soil. Kale is among the many seeds that lend themselves to being sown as microgreens since they germinate and grow relatively quickly.

All the vitamins, minerals and phytonutrients present in grown-up kale plants are available in microgreens, and they can be raised easily and adapted to many situations. Much of the year they can be grown outdoors on balconies, windowsills, and in the tiniest of spaces. Raising these mini veggie gardens is a perfect project for kids both at home or in the classroom.

You will need a lot of seed to grow microgreens because they are sown much more thickly than they would be to raise a kale plant—you more or less crowd the seeds in the planting medium in order to be able to harvest enough microgreens to make a mouthful.

Most regular kale seed packages don't contain sufficient quantities for this, so the best source would be your own saved seed. I have noticed that some Italian seed companies offer generous amounts of seed in their packages—I take advantage of this often.

It's important to note that very occasionally certain seeds are treated with chemicals like thiram to ward off pests that would interfere with germination and early growth. To me, these seeds would be unsuitable for sowing as microgreens. The package will clearly state that the seeds have been treated; my consideration is that when you eat microgreens it's possible that you'd ingest the root that has been in close contact with a pesticide.

If you don't have your own going-to-seed kale plants yet—and you will find you can harvest a *lot* of seed from one large kale plant when you do—many seed companies are now catering to microgreen growers and offering bigger quantities per package.

Starting your adventures with microgreens is as easy as getting your hands on a large, shallow black seeding tray, available from many nurseries for a nominal charge. You are, of course, not limited to these rudimentary but functional containers; any other pot or container can be used as well. Shallow pots made for bonsai are attractive when sown with microgreens; ditto shallow or even deep woven or wooden baskets or boxes when lined with coir, paper towels, landscape fabric or even opened-up coffee filters to keep the soil from falling out.

As the tiny greens need very little soil to grow, place 1 to 2 inches (2.5–5 cm) of planting medium, preferably decently rich, in the container, and sow seed thickly. After that, water lightly with a spray bottle. Place the container in a location with good light and air circulation, then keep moist by misting frequently until the seeds germinate.

You *can* grow microgreens in perlite, vermiculite or other soil substitutes, but in order to produce a good result, fertilizing would be necessary, so instead stick to good-quality soil purchased from a garden centre.

Kale flower, chive and allium make a charming bouquet. *iStock photo*

If the light is insufficient, your kale microgreens will get "leggy"—meaning they will stretch towards the light. Because kale doesn't mind cold temperatures, put your microgreens outdoors in the full available light as soon as possible, preferably within a day or two of sprouting.

To enjoy your tiny greens, trim with scissors. You can cut the "seed" leaves—the little heart-shaped ones—but if you do that, the greens won't regrow. Since the "true" leaf stage is reached pretty quickly—usually within a week or ten days of sowing, better to wait so you can enjoy your tiny greens for a longer period of time. Like "cut-and-come-again" greens described on page 28, your microgreens can be fed with a quarter- or half-strength liquid organic feed, and will regrow several times for your munching enjoyment!

For ways to enjoy your tiny greens, see Turkey Burgers with Microgreens (page 172), toss them into salads, sandwiches and smoothies, or just eat them out of hand.

GUERILLA GARDENING WITH KALE

Or, ways to be generous with this generous plant!

Make seed "bombs" (or if you prefer, seed "balls") to toss onto barren areas of public soil or to give away.

Centaurea montana, or glory-of-the-snow, isn't edible, but it's a favourite with honeybees. *Heather Neilsen photo*

Since you'll need lots of kale seed for this, your own saved seeds would be ideal.

YOU'LL NEED:
- Clay (from an art-supply store)
- Some compost or lightweight garden soil
- Lots of kale seeds

Red clay gives them a pretty colour, but any clay is fine. Using one part clay to two parts soil or dry compost, and however many seeds you wish, mix everything in a bowl or bucket, adding enough water to bind. Shape into "golf balls." Kids love this job. Allow your "bombs" to dry on paper towels or newspaper.

Instead of wildflower seeds, make kale-seed packages for guests at weddings. You can include the story of the Scottish lassies (page 19) for those who might not catch the bridal bouquet. Grow kale on your boulevard or front yard; display a sign telling people to help themselves. Add a "factsheet" about kale and post it nearby.

In a nutshell, start a tradition of sharing kale seeds, and inspire others to do the same.

MAKE A GARDEN FOR POLLINATING INSECTS

According to the Wild Garden Seeds catalogue, kale is a "great insectary plant, attracting beneficial wasps, syrphid flies, lady beetles, lacewings and other general predators. . ."

Besides kale, here's a list of plants to include in your insectary garden to help the pollinators, including the precious bees that are so important to our food supply.

HERBS
Cilantro, parsley, fennel, dill, marjoram, mint, oregano, thyme, chamomile

VEGGIES
Carrots (let a few go to seed—this happens in the second year), beans (pole, bush and scarlet runner), broad beans

FLOWERS
Alyssum, cosmos, California poppies, sea holly, wild roses, yarrow, alliums, tulips, crocus, evening primrose, bachelor's buttons, coreopsis, feverfew, goldenrod, hollyhocks, glory-of-the-snow and many more

WEEDS
Dandelions, buttercups, chickweed, clover

COVER CROPS
Buckwheat, phacelia ('Bee's Friend')

WATCH THE BIRDIE

Some birds, such as finches, use kale plants as perches in the garden. While they're hopping about on the plants, they nibble flowers and tender top leaves; it's fun to watch kale stems move up and down like teeter-totters.

KALE IN CONTAINERS

Last but not least, show kids how kale can look good in the vase, on its own or mixed with flowers and other greenery—this would make a great gift for mom on Mother's Day or for a special teacher at the end of the school year. Be sure to change the water daily.

Some Varieties of Kale to Grow

The botanical name for kale is *Brassica oleracea acephala*, meaning cabbage without a head. Another common name other than "kale"—often heard in England—is "borecole." Kale is a member of the cruciferous family of vegetables, which also includes broccoli, cauliflower, cabbage, Asian greens, rapini, Brussels sprouts, kohlrabi, radishes and more.

Apparently, *Brassica oleraceae* also branches out into another division, known as *Brassica napus*, which includes the "Pabularia" group known as Siberian or Russian kale. *B. oleraceae* includes broad-leafed varieties like 'Lacinato', also called Tuscan, dinosaur, black palm, palm, black kale, and probably other names as well.

Why dinosaur kale? Maybe that nickname came about because kale's skin is bumpy like our idea of dinosaur's skin. Or possibly because dinosaurs may have eaten kale, since there is some evidence that a form of kale may have existed millions of years ago. Palm is yet another nickname because when lower leaves are picked, the plant slightly resembles a palm tree. Black, because the leaves are darker; there are some varieties in Italy that are much darker and which the Italians call cavolo nero (literally, black cabbage).

The term "laciniate" refers to "having a fringe" or "slashed into narrow pointed lobes"—neither of these really fits the Tuscan kale (to me) as it's not fringed, nor is it slashed. Confusion about plant names is nothing new, as is very well illustrated by this excerpt from the *Journal of Practical Horticulture* (1869), written by "Anonymous"...

> *In referring to catalogues, I find Chou de Milan, Buda, Egyptian, and Jerusalem Kale all candidates for the name Asparagus Kale. No doubt they are all sprouting Kales, and this must be their principal advantage, but which of them should be called the Asparagus Kale? Some authority ought to speak out, so that the trade may be somewhat agreed. In the spring I asked Mr. Duncan Hairs if he could put me right about Asparagus Kale. He said he knew the Kale well, and would give me a pinch of seed. I sowed it, and it proved to be Jerusalem Kale according to Cattell, and certainly at the present moment about its shoot there is more that would claim the cognomen "Asparagus" than the varieties of other Kales I have just named. Mr. Barr, from another source, received seed as Lapland Kale, which proved also to be Jerusalem Kale. He also received some seed as Miller's Winter Kale, which proved to be Egyptian Kale. From a third seedsman he had Ragged Jack, an upright somewhat laciniated Kale. He had the same Kale from another source as Bagged Jack.*

Broad-leafed varieties like 'Lacinato' are also called Tuscan, dinosaur, black palm, palm, black kale and more. *Vivian Evans photo*

A raised bed planted up with Swiss chard, Russian kale and chives. *Carol Pope photo*

Tuscan and curly. *Vilseskogen photo*

The "Ragged" or "Bagged Jack" noted above likely refers to a 'Red Russian' type that self-seeds like there's no tomorrow and withstands very cold temperatures. Perhaps that's because it's related to Siberian kale.

And on it goes. There are other far older varieties too—Scots kale has been around for thousands of years, and comes in umpteen forms. All kale can be sweet, especially when grown in winter months, and most varieties can be used interchangeably in cooking. With the growing popularity of kale, expect to see more types on the market—in stores, and in seed catalogues, bred to be sweeter, to grow faster, thrive in colder or hotter weather, or offer unusual or different colouration, and more or less frilliness, making it all the more beautiful for your yard and tasty for your plate.

There seems to be a mind-boggling list of curly kale seed available, including 'Afro', 'Winterbor', 'Starbor', 'Blueridge', 'Dwarf Blue Curled' and 'Westlandse Winter', to name a few. These are very curly kales, having been bred using the Scottish variety or varieties.

'Ripbor' F1 is a super-vigorous compact version of the curly kales. 'Darkibor' F1, similar but a little taller, pairs nicely in the garden with 'Redbor' F1, as they are about the same size and shape but form a beautiful colour contrast.

If you want red- or red/purple-toned veggies in your garden, grow 'Red Ursa', 'Winter Red' or 'RedBor' F1.

And there are more kales of various colours, size small, medium, large and extra-large, with flat leaves, curly leaves, even white leaves with a bit of green. All await you—just check out the reliable seed suppliers listed at the end of this book. Please note that not all varieties of kale on offer are listed, and some suppliers have many others as well.

Opposite page (L–R): (first row) 'Redbor' F1. *Nick Saltmarsh photo*; 'Rainbow Tuscan'. *Sharon Hanna photo*; (second row) Scottish. *Sharon Hanna photo*; 'Red Russian'. *Derek Visser photo*; (third row) 'Blueridge'. *Quinn Dombrowski photo*; 'Winterbor'. *Sharon Hanna photo*

RECIPES

How to Cook with Kale

HARVESTING FROM THE GARDEN

Although cooking with kale isn't rocket science, if you grow your own kale (and I hope you do!) it should be mentioned that older leaves are suitable for use in soups and stews, kalekopita, kale chips or anything with longer cooking times. Newer leaves from the top of the plant or side shoots are best for quick cooking or salads.

In winter and early spring after kale has frozen and thawed a few times, the stems become edible, even delicious—a little like asparagus. Thinner, tender stems can be chopped and used along with the leaves in any recipe. Thicker ones can be peeled like a carrot, chopped up and thrown into soups or stir-fries.

STORE-BOUGHT KALE

If you are buying kale, your first choice should be organic and locally grown. In fact, hopefully you are using as many organically grown veggies as possible! Organic markets usually carry decent kale. In the past, that kale has frequently been the curly green kind, but these days it's often the Tuscan variety, the current darling of cooks. It seems reasonable that as kale grows in popularity by leaps and bounds, more types of kale will find their way to the produce shelves, and we might want to encourage produce managers to try their best to find local growers, especially in winter.

Whatever you find, remember that *any* kale is better than none. Choose fresh, sturdy leaves and get them into the fridge as soon as possible. Or eat them right away—nutrients are lost once the leaves are picked, as with all vegetables, so the quicker they find their way to your table, the better.

IN THE KITCHEN

Kale leaves tolerate more time in the pot than thinner greens like chard and spinach, which can easily be overcooked. They can also be steamed lightly for a few minutes and drizzled with a little olive oil or butter if you like, or served plain. Toss them into almost any soup or stew, and add them to pasta dishes including lasagna. Yes, you can even add kale to Kraft Dinner—we won't tell.

Enjoy kale raw by adding a few leaves, buds or flowers to your favourite salad. Buds are great for dipping and easy for kids to handle.

ABOUT KALE VARIETIES

In produce departments, restaurants, magazines, newspapers and seed catalogues, you are likely to see Tuscan, dinosaur, 'Lacinato', palm and black kale, and possibly more names. They are basically the same type of kale—broad-leafed, not curly and usually much darker, originating (we think) in Italy. In the recipe section, I have called it Tuscan for simplicity, though Tuscan is not an actual named cultivar. Tuscan kale leaves are thought to be a little more tender, making this type suitable for raw or barely cooked/sautéed dishes.

WASTE NOT

You might notice some harping about not discarding kale's cooking water, for which I apologize in advance, but it's just too good to pour down the drain. Let it cool and drink it like herbal tea or mix it with tomato or V8 juice—if you don't think it's delicious at first, you'll acquire a taste for it, as I did. If you have a large jar or plastic container that fits in your freezer, use it to collect and store small amounts of your kale broth for later use in soups or for cooking quinoa, rice or pasta.

And, speaking of broth—nothing quite equals homemade stock or broth of any kind, be it chicken, vegetable or kale. But sometimes homemade isn't an option. My preference when it comes to a chicken-stock substitute is the concentrated soup paste Better Than Bouillon. In my opinion it has more flavour than the ready-made liquid stocks that often seem watered down. As my dear father used to say, "they ran that chicken through there pretty fast." Take care when using BTB—stick to the instructions, diluting as indicated. Have a taste of the almost-finished product before you add extra salt.

MEASURING KALE

If you are buying kale, it's usually sold in a bunch, weighing somewhere around a pound or 454 grams. To my reckoning, this much kale equals something like 8 to 10 cups (about 2 L) of leaves, tightly packed in a large measuring cup. Of course, it depends on the age of the kale, the size of the leaves, how big the stems are, etc. And you can always go ahead and use a little *extra*, because more is a good thing when it comes to kale, and virtually all these recipes could accommodate a titch more.

AS YOU BEGIN COOKING. . .

All recipes assume washing of vegetables before using, and removing any hard or fibrous stem parts. When cutting away kale ribs and stems, see if you can find a use for them. Toss them into the freezer for later use in soups or veggie broths. Or feed them to your chickens or someone else's—chickens love kale and eating it contributes greatly to the quality of their eggs.

A FEW THOUGHTS ON INGREDIENTS

Some recipes call for cheese, and sometimes Parmigiano, which some people might call Parmesan. There is Reggiano—the most expensive—and Padano, which costs less and has a similar flavour but is less intense. There is a version of Romano (proper name: Pecorino Romano) in every little town and village in Tuscany. Asiago is one of my favourites—it's relatively inexpensive and to me has the flavour of a younger Parmigiano. Piave is yet

another hard, strong cheese. All of these work fine in any of the recipes that call for Parmigiano, so feel free to use your favourite.

A number of recipes call for butter, sometimes both butter and olive oil, during the sautéing process. If you prefer the vegan style of eating, just substitute oil for butter. When it comes to mashed potatoes (in Stampot and other recipes), if you'd like to replace the butter with a substitute, please do—but I cannot guarantee the taste will be the same.

When I mention black pepper, I'm thinking of freshly ground, and if a recipe calls for olive oil, I mean extra virgin. Organic would be nice too, but it seems that many olive-oil manufacturers in Europe would shudder at the use of pesticides on their precious olive trees, so the term may just be at least partly redundant—let's hope so, anyway.

Bon appétit!

ABOUT THE SYMBOLS

These symbols help identify recipes suitable to your (or your guests) dietary preferences:

GF = Gluten-free

VG = Vegetarian

VE = Vegan

* = Gluten-free, vegetarian or vegan with modification

"CHIFFONADE"

Many recipes indicate that kale leaves should be "in chiffonade." The technique comes from the French, and is also commonly used with other leafy vegetables and herbs such as basil. It refers to a way of rolling a few leaves at a time tightly together, the way tobacco leaves are rolled into a cigar. After rolling the leaves, a sharp knife is used to slice the roll into thin sections as you would slice a baguette, straight or on the diagonal. When unrolled, the "chiffonade" method yields thin pieces that cook quickly or are perfect for salads.

Of course, it makes sense to roll the flatter-leafed or slightly curled kales, and not the super-curly ones that would be difficult to roll up tightly. If curly kale is to be chopped, just grab it with one hand firmly, squeeze it a little, and cut it as you would chop parsley—coarsely for stews and stir-fries, finer for other dishes like salads and slaws.

BREAKFAST

On the Power of Smoothies

Additions to your kale smoothie:

Avocado

Cucumber

Blueberries

Apples

Pears

Grapes

Orange juice

Grapefruit juice

For extra zing, add:

Lemon

Freshly chopped ginger root

Goji berries

Tiny pinch of cayenne

Carol Pope, my wonderful editor, has allowed me to share this remarkable Tale of Smoothies:

As a little guy, our son had terrible allergies to the point that he would go through a box of Kleenex a day. We took him to an allergist who tested him and said he was allergic to a ton of things including cheese and dogs, which made him weep a little—he loved pizza and really wanted a puppy, so this was all terrible news. The doctor suggested a course of allergy shots for him, but at that point, his dad pointed out that our son's allergies could all be the result of his staunch refusal to eat vegetables (except where I could sneak bits into spaghetti or soup). So his dad started experimenting with smoothie recipes loaded with every vegetable he could get his hands on, including and especially a lot of kale. It took a while and many experiments but he persevered and finally found a formula that our son and his sisters enjoyed (almost) enough to happily drink about 6 to 8 oz (180 to 250 mL) every morning.

After a month, all of our son's allergies were COMPLETELY *gone. As the mom, I also drank the juice to show how 'delicious' it was. Well, at first it wasn't, but with time and practice, my husband was serving up good-tasting green juice. The secret, he says, is you have to add enough banana and lemon to smooth it all out.*

If you already have a favourite smoothie recipe, try adding a little chopped fresh kale. The very pretty pale-green smoothie pictured contains kale, banana, yogurt, a little honey and a few ice cubes.

Green Queen Smoothie

1 cup (250 mL) green
grapes, washed

½ ripe 'Bartlett' pear

1 cup (250 mL) kale leaves

½ cup (125 mL) water

½ cup (125 mL) yogurt

A few ice cubes

In a blender or food processor, combine all ingredients. Process until smooth, then enjoy!

SERVES TWO

Simple Kale Frittata

2 eggs

¼ cup (60 mL) water

Salt and black pepper to taste

2 tsp (10 mL) oil or butter

Finely chopped purple or yellow onion

Minced garlic (optional)

1 cup (250 mL) kale leaves in chiffonade

¼ cup (60 mL) grated cheese—Asiago, cheddar, Jarlsberg or your favourite

Worried about my lack of appetite in the a.m., my mother squeezed fresh orange juice for me every morning of my elementary-school life. To give me protein, she secretly added a raw egg yolk to the orange juice and stirred it furiously, but I knew something was strange about my juice. Every morning I drank it, then felt awful. Somewhere around Grade 5, I caught my mom red-handed, holding the eggshells, and the jig was up. This is a much more palatable rendition of eggs—with kale and cheese. I like to eat this at room temperature or cold.

Whisk eggs in a small bowl with water, salt and pepper until light.

In a non-stick frying pan, heat the oil or butter over medium heat. Add onion and sauté until slightly softened, 1 or 2 minutes. Add garlic (if desired) and kale. Continue to stir and cook 5 minutes—kale should be wilted but still bright green.

Add egg mixture to the pan and turn heat to medium-low. Allow eggs to cook to desired degree of firmness. If you are an expert at flipping, flip the kale/egg mixture (it's good to have an audience for this). When eggs are almost cooked to your liking, add the cheese. Serve hot or warm.

SERVES ONE

Savoury Kale Scones with Pumpkin & Cheese

2 cups (475 mL) kale leaves, loosely packed

2 cups (475 mL) unbleached flour

½ tsp (2.5 mL) salt

1 tsp (5 mL) baking soda

½ tsp (2.5 mL) baking powder

1 Tbsp (15 mL) sugar

⅓ cup (80 mL) cold butter

1 egg

¾ cup (180 mL) buttermilk

½ cup (125 mL) cooked squash or pumpkin in small dice

¾ cup (180 mL) cheddar cheese, grated

Whether you pronounce them "skawns" or "skownes" these are great in the morning, and leftovers are yummy with homemade soup. Or make tiny scones, cut-out with a fancy cookie cutter, for hors d'oeuvres.

These are dropped by the spoonful but if you'd rather use a cookie cutter or knife to make triangles or other shapes, knead in about ¼ cup (60 mL) of extra flour at the end to make the dough easier to handle.

Preheat oven to 375F (190C). Set oven rack in the middle.

Steam kale for a minute or two, just to blanch. Chop kale finely, squeezing out as much liquid as you can. You should have less than 1 cup (250 mL) of chopped kale. If you have more, save it for soup or eat it. (Too much will make the scones sticky.)

Blend or sift the flour, salt, soda, baking powder and sugar together. Cut in the butter with a pastry blender or your fingers.

In a small bowl, beat the egg, then add the buttermilk, continuing to beat until well combined. Add egg/buttermilk mixture, along with squash, kale and cheese to dry ingredients, mixing with a fork just enough to combine.

Drop by spoonfuls onto parchment-paper-covered cookie sheet. Bake about 20 minutes until lightly browned.

MAKES EIGHT TO TEN LARGE SCONES

Savoury Kale Muffins

2 eggs

1 cup (250 mL) cottage cheese

1 tsp (5 mL) dried dillweed

3 Tbsp (45 mL) minced onion, shallots or chives

Pinch cayenne

3 cups (700 mL) kale leaves, loosely packed

1½ cups (350 mL) flour

1 tsp (5 mL) baking powder

½ tsp (2.5 mL) salt

Cheese (optional) for topping

These are very moist, and a little like a crumpet—the inspiration for these muffins being the cottage-cheese muffin at Solly's, a neighbourhood bagelry. Serve at breakfast, brunch or lunch with soup, or make tiny blobs on a cookie sheet to serve as an hors d'oeuvre. They are quite green, so perfect with green eggs and ham or for St. Patrick's Day.

In a medium bowl, beat eggs until foamy. Add cottage cheese, dillweed, onion and cayenne, mixing only to combine.

Preheat oven to 375F (190C).

Place kale in the bowl of a food processor. Pulse a couple of times until the kale is chopped very finely. Squeeze excess moisture from the kale and add to cheese mixture.

In a medium bowl, sift flour, baking powder and salt. Add wet mixture to dry ingredients, stirring only enough to blend—a few lumps are okay. Spoon into greased or non-stick muffin pans. Add a small piece of cheese to the top of each muffin if desired.

Bake about 20 minutes or until tops are lightly browned.

MAKES TWELVE MUFFINS

Breakfast Okonomiyaki

*

1 large egg

⅓ cup (80 mL) water

Pinch of salt

Dash of tamari

2 Tbsp (30 mL) flour

¼ tsp (1 mL) baking powder

Black pepper

1 heaping cup (250 mL) kale and other veggies, slivered or cut with a mandoline

2 tsp (10 ml) vegetable oil

*with gluten-free tamari, flour and baking powder

My Japanese students made this dish, often using cabbage, pork and onions—and it's traditionally decorated with brown sauce and Japanese mayo from squeeze bottles. A quick and nutritious option to carbo-type breakfasts, this recipe yields one 8-inch (20-cm) round and you can use 2 eggs if you like.

With a good combination of veggies—kale, a bit of orange squash grated on a box grater, cabbage, onion and cilantro, it's a beautiful way to start the day. It's also a great way to use up leftover potatoes, sweet potatoes or yams. Always include at least one member of the *Brassica* family—kale! These make nice appetizers too if you make them bite-sized. To make this recipe gluten-free, use non-gluten flour, tamari and baking powder.

Beat egg with water. Add salt and tamari, then stir in the flour, baking powder and pepper. Add veggies and mix until they're well coated. Heat a non-stick pan to medium and add the oil. When the pan is heated, spoon or pour your okonomiyaki into the pan to make a flattish circle.

Cook about 4 minutes per side. Towards the end of the cooking time, cover the pan to ensure vegetables are cooked through.

MAKES ONE

Kale, Bacon & Potato Frittata

½ lb (225 gr) lean smoky bacon, cut in ½-inch (1.25-cm) strips

2 cups (475 mL) onion, halved and thinly sliced

10 cups (2.4 L) kale—about 1 lb (454 gr), chopped

8 eggs

½ tsp (2.5 mL) salt

Black pepper

1 cup (250 mL) Parmigiano-Reggiano, grated, divided

1⅓ cups (about 400 mL) ricotta cheese

This is a full-on, bacon-y pie and not for the faint of heart. You need to go for a long walk before or after this one, as there are no herbs and nothing light or garden-y (aside from kale, of course) included. But at least it does contain kale—and lots of it.

In an ideal world, you have a large heavy-bottomed ovenproof non-stick skillet. That's a lot to ask, though, so ovenproof and skillet are the two operative words. In that pan, cook the bacon until crisp. Save the drippings in a small bowl, drain bacon on paper towels and set aside.

Pour some drippings back into the skillet, and sauté the onions over medium heat for about 5 minutes. Add some of the kale, cook down until it wilts, then add the rest. Turn the heat to low, and sauté until the kale is tender, about 10 minutes. Transfer kale to a large plate, spreading it to cool a little.

Clean the skillet. (That sounds bossy, doesn't it?) In a large bowl, beat the eggs well with the salt and pepper. Add half of the Parmigiano-Reggiano, all the kale, and the bacon. Add the ricotta but don't mix it too much—it's nice to have a few bits separate throughout the frittata.

Preheat oven to 350F (175C). Heat 1 Tbsp (15 mL) of the bacon drippings in the pan over medium heat. Add the egg, kale and cheese mixture, spreading out evenly. Sprinkle the rest of the cheese over the top. Cook for 10 minutes until the edges begin to come away from the pan, then bake for about 15 minutes or until the frittata is set and/or done to your liking. Using a flexible heat-proof spatula, loosen the frittata and transfer to a platter. Cut in wedges and serve warm or at room temperature.

SERVES SIX

STARTERS & LIGHT MEALS

Kale Chips

Washed kale leaves—to fit baking pan in a single layer

Olive, avocado, walnut or grapeseed oil

Sea or kosher salt

Bragg Liquid Aminos or tamari soy sauce

Sesame seeds

Parchment paper

*with gluten-free soy sauce

You can buy these delicate, high-priced treats—but by the time you get them home they're often in tiny bits. Since they don't travel well, make your own—it's a snap!

You can dry kale in the oven or in a dehydrator. A dehydrator takes longer but may dry the chips more evenly. Large older/thicker leaves work well. Because its leaves are relatively flat and tend to dry evenly, 'Lacinato' can be left whole as pictured, without removing the stem. Still, any variety of kale can successfully be made into chips. If you prefer to go gluten-free, use Bragg Liquid Aminos or a gluten-free soy sauce.

Rub one or both sides of leaves lightly with oil, sprinkle with salt, adding a dash or spray of Bragg's or soy sauce if desired. Sprinkle with sesame seeds. Having said this, you can dry the kale leaves completely plain, especially if you think kids might prefer them unadorned, with maybe just a little salt. Experiment with other seasonings—barbecue spice, Spike, prepared rubs or a smidgen of garlic salt.

IN THE OVEN: Preheat the oven to 325F (160C). Place rack in the middle of the oven. Lay the leaves out whole, or in smaller pieces, on a baking pan lined with parchment paper. Bake for 10 minutes and check to ensure they're toasting evenly, then continue baking, checking every 5 minutes or so. The leaves should feel overall dry to the touch but should not shatter. If they do, use the bits for Kale and Cranberry Crisps (page 74) or Kale Gomasio (page 76).

IN THE DEHYDRATOR: To dry kale in a dehydrator, dry as per the usual directions. My dehydrator is very rudimentary with just a small element and no fan, and the kale takes quite a while to dry. Keep checking every hour or so until the kale is adequately dehydrated (as per above).

SERVES TWO TO FOUR

Kale & Cranberry Crisps

Parchment paper

1 medium bunch (4 cups or 1 L) Tuscan kale

1 tsp (5 mL) peanut or coconut oil

¼ cup (60 mL) buttermilk

2 Tbsp (30 mL) molasses

¼ cup (60 mL) pecans

¼ cup (60 mL) sunflower seeds or hulled pumpkin seeds

¼ cup (60 mL) flax seeds

¼ cup (60 mL) sesame seeds

¼ cup (60 mL) poppy seeds

¼ cup (60 mL) dried sweetened cranberries

1 small sprig rosemary, finely chopped

1 tsp (5 mL) salt

1 tsp (5 mL) baking soda

2 Tbsp (30 mL) brown sugar

½ cup (125 mL) flour

Kale and cranberries come together beautifully in this rustic cracker. If you don't have a food processor, never fear—just chop the ingredients, then combine by hand. The parchment paper, however, is essential.

Preheat oven to 425F (220C) and line a large baking sheet with parchment.

Toss kale leaves in oil and lay out in a single layer on the baking sheet. Bake for 8 to 10 minutes until crisp but still bright green. Set aside to cool and turn oven down to 250F (105C).

In a small saucepan, combine buttermilk and molasses. Whisk over low heat until well mixed and set aside to cool.

Combine dry ingredients and crispy kale in food processor and pulse a few times until pecans and larger nuts are finely chopped but still distinct. In two batches, combine wet ingredients into dry and pulse briefly, just until a dough forms.

Transfer dough to a large parchment-lined baking sheet, then top with a second sheet of parchment (feel free to reuse the parchment from the first step). With a rolling pin, roll out dough to a thickness of about ⅛ inch (3 mm).

Bake for 30 minutes, then remove the top layer of parchment and turn off heat, leaving crisps in the oven for 8 hours. When the time is up, cut or break the crisps into pieces and store in an airtight tin or bag until needed. These are especially delicious as part of a cheese course.

MAKES ABOUT TWO DOZEN 2-INCH (5-CM) CRISPS

Kale Gomasio

⅓ cup (80 mL) pumpkin seeds, preferably organic

¼ cup (60 mL) black sesame seeds

¼ cup (60 mL) natural or white sesame seeds

⅓ cup (80 mL) flaked dried kale

¼ cup (60 mL) sea or kosher salt

1 Tbsp (15 mL) flaked dulse or other seaweed (optional)

Dried orange or lemon zest (optional)

When you're making kale chips, save some overly crispy bits to make gomasio—a kind of salt substitute used in Japan, usually made of sesame seeds and salt. Sprinkle gomasio on salads, veggies, rice, popcorn or anywhere you fancy. This version tastes a little like Spike, with the added nutrition of seaweed and kale.

Use a small cast-iron frying pan if you have one. If not, any heavy-bottomed pan is fine.

Toast pumpkin seeds lightly over medium-low heat for a few minutes in a dry pan, shaking often. Add the sesame seeds and toast a few minutes more, watching and stirring the mixture to ensure it doesn't burn.

Process the toasted seeds with the dried kale, salt, seaweed flakes and zest in the small bowl of a food processor until you have a coarse powder (most of the sesame seeds will remain whole).

MAKES 1 GENEROUS CUP (250 ML)

Fermented Kale with Ginger & Miso

½ small green cabbage

1 cup (250 mL) packed kale leaves

1 small carrot, peeled and cut into thin slivers

Sea salt

2 tsp (10 mL) fresh ginger root, minced

2 cloves garlic, minced

1 Tbsp (15 mL) miso (fermented soybean paste)

*with gluten-free miso

Like yogurt, fermented vegetables are thought to contain bacteria beneficial for the stomach. In my Gaia College "Growing Food in the City" class, we made fermented cabbage with everyone lending a (clean) hand. It's a kind of kimchi without the heat, and is easy and fun to make. Add daikon if you prefer it a little spicier. I like to eat fermented veggies as a snack any time of the day, or with rice at lunch or dinner. It's also good with steamed or sautéed fish.

After scrubbing up, be sure to rinse hands very well so that no trace of soap smell remains.

Lightly rinse the cabbage (outside only). Give the kale only a perfunctory rinse to get rid of spiderwebs, etc. The beneficial bacteria that creates the fermentation is contained on the outside of the vegetables and you don't want to wash it all off.

Slice the cabbage and kale thinly, place in a bowl with the carrots, add about ½ Tbsp (7.5 mL) of salt and begin to massage/rub the salt vigorously into the vegetables. In a few moments the veggies will begin to release their liquid. Add a little more salt and continue to rub the pieces well with your hands. When more liquid appears, add the ginger root, garlic and miso, and mix well.

Let the bowl sit on your kitchen counter, covered with a plate, for about 48 hours. It should smell slightly fermented, a little like beer. Transfer the mixture into a clean jar fitted with a lid, and store in the fridge. It will keep for a couple of months.

MAKES ABOUT 2 CUPS (475 ML)

Sunshine Coast Salad Rolls with Kale & Wild Mushrooms

8 oz (225 gr) fresh wild mushrooms (a combination of chanterelle and hedgehog is excellent)

2 Tbsp (30 mL) peanut oil or olive oil

2 Tbsp (30 mL) fresh ginger, minced

3 cloves garlic, minced

½ tsp (2.5 mL) red pepper flakes or black pepper

Pinch of salt

1 small bunch scallions, chopped

1 tsp (5 mL) soy sauce

About a dozen 12-inch (30-cm) or sixteen 8-inch (20-cm) rice-paper spring-roll wrappers—plus a few extra in case some tear

2 cups (475 mL) young kale leaves in chiffonade (or use your preferred combination of kale, beet greens, chard and other greens)

6 oz (170 gr) bean-thread noodles, or brown-rice vermicelli noodles, cooked to package directions, drained, rinsed and tossed with 1½ Tbsp (20 mL) seasoned rice vinegar

1 small carrot, in matchstick pieces

About 2 dozen sprigs of cilantro or basil leaves

*with gluten-free soy sauce

Combining the taste of mushrooms and kale, this vegetarian variation on a Vietnamese salad roll makes an inexpensive appetizer or light lunch for a crowd. It might take a couple of tries to get the knack of the rice-paper wrappers, but trust me, it's not hard. Rice-paper spring-roll wrappers are usually available in the Asian section of supermarkets in 8-inch (20-cm) and 12-inch (30-cm) diameters. The smaller wraps are better for appetizers, but more fiddly to use. If you get skunked (literally or figuratively) in your search for edible wild mushrooms, store-bought oyster mushrooms are equally delectable.

First, prepare the mushrooms. If you're using wild mushrooms, they'll likely need to be cleaned of pine needles and grit. Disregard any warnings you've heard on the perils of getting mushrooms wet and give them a thorough rinse under cold running water to remove any debris. Shake off excess water and roughly chop. Place a large skillet over high heat (without oil) until very hot, then add the freshly washed mushrooms—don't worry about drying them first. Cook over high heat, stirring occasionally until most of the water has evaporated and the mushrooms begin to stick to the pan. Immediately reduce heat to medium low then add oil, ginger and garlic, pepper and pinch of salt. Stirring occasionally, cook until mushrooms are tender and slightly crispy around the edges, then add scallions and soy sauce and cook for another minute. Set mushrooms aside to cool.

Over

Continued from previous page.

TO ASSEMBLE THE ROLLS: In a shallow bowl or large skillet soak a spring-roll wrapper in hot water until very pliable, 45 seconds to a minute. Move the softened wrapper to your work surface and add another wrapper to the water to soak while you assemble the first roll.

Carefully spread a wrapper so it does not rip. Arrange a small handful of greens on the bottom half of the wrapper, leaving a 1-inch (2.5-cm) border along bottom edge and sides. Top with a spoonful of the cooked mushrooms, then a small handful of noodles, a sprinkling of carrots and a couple sprigs of cilantro or basil leaves. Fold the bottom up over the filling, fold the sides in and then roll tightly. If the roll rips, use a second sheet of rice paper to double wrap and use a little less filling for the next roll.

Repeat, placing rolls in a plastic bag, or in a resealable container covered with a damp paper towel until ready to eat. Rolls can be made up to a day ahead. Before serving, slice rolls in half diagonally, then serve with peanut sauce (next page) for dipping.

SERVES FOUR AS A LIGHT LUNCH, OR EIGHT AS AN APPETIZER

Super All-Purpose Peanut Sauce

1 Tbsp (15 mL) peanut, vegetable or coconut oil

3 cloves garlic, minced

2 Tbsp (30 mL) fresh ginger, minced

1–4 red chili peppers, chopped, or 1 tsp (5 mL) hot sauce or red pepper flakes

⅓ cup (75 mL) natural peanut butter

Juice of 1 lime or 2 Tbsp (30 mL) seasoned rice vinegar

¼ cup (60 mL) coconut milk, water or beer

2 Tbsp (30 mL) brown sugar or honey

1 Tbsp (15 mL) sesame oil

1 Tbsp (15 mL) soy sauce

*vegan if brown sugar is used, gluten-free if non-gluten soy sauce is used

Adapted, with thanks, from the recipe in James Barber's *One-Pot Wonders* (Harbour Publishing, 2006). This sauce keeps for several days in the fridge and, in addition to being a natural complement to salad rolls, makes a simple meal of rice and greens quite wonderful. Barber suggests using up to 4 chili peppers—but if you're making this for young children, you may want to skip them altogether.

Heat oil in small saucepan over medium-high. Sauté garlic, ginger and chili until golden brown and fragrant. Add remaining ingredients and, whisking, bring to a boil. Reduce heat to low and simmer, continuing to whisk, until thickened.

MAKES ABOUT 1 CUP (250 ML)

Lemony Kale & Goat Cheese Dip

 *

About 2 cups (475 mL) kale
leaves, chopped

1 small onion or shallot, minced

2 garlic cloves, whole

¾ cup (180 mL) fresh goat cheese

Juice of small lemon

1 tsp (5 mL) lemon zest

¼ tsp (1 mL) sea salt

½ tsp (2.5 mL) rosemary,
finely minced

Pinch cayenne

*if served with corn chips, rice
crackers or vegetables

Serve with crudités, crackers, bread, pita chips, or other crispy snacks like my very favourite tortilla chips, Fresh is Best, out of Kamloops, BC. The chips are so fresh and authentic-tasting that they've become very popular and widely available. I was fortunate enough to try them at the Saturday Kamloops Farmers' Market about five years ago, before they went big time. I admit that I returned to the sample table to appreciate their chips and dip again and again—until it got a little embarrassing!

Since this recipe is reminiscent of certain types of spinach dip, it's a good way to initiate a kale non-believer.

In a large saucepan, combine kale, onion, garlic and ½ cup (125 mL) water. Set over medium heat, cover and cook, stirring occasionally, until vegetables are tender—about 8 minutes. Attend to the pan, adding a little water if needed.

Transfer to food processor; let stand and cool for a few minutes. Add goat cheese, lemon juice and zest, salt, rosemary and cayenne; process until smooth.

MAKES ABOUT 2 CUPS (475 ML)

Kale Hummus with Toasted Almonds

3 cups (700 mL) kale leaves

4 large garlic cloves, whole, unpeeled

½ cup (125 mL) frozen green peas

⅓ cup (80 mL) almonds

¼ cup (60 mL) peanut butter

½ tsp (2.5 mL) salt

¼ tsp (1 mL) ground black pepper

1 tsp (5 mL) sugar

Juice of ½ lemon

2 cups (475 mL) cooked chickpeas, rinsed

¼ cup (60 mL) olive oil

From my point of view, hummus is absolutely begging to have kale added to it. Made quickly in your food processor, this kale-y version is a beautiful shade of pea green and a calcium powerhouse. If you prefer, use tahini or another nut butter in place of the peanut butter.

Cook kale in about 1 cup (250 mL) of water for about 5 minutes, until slightly tender but still green. Using a slotted spoon, remove kale and drain.

Add unpeeled garlic cloves to kale cooking water. Cover and boil gently about 5 minutes. Add peas and cook 2 to 3 minutes until they are tender and bright green. Drain peas, retaining ½ cup (125 mL) cooking liquid for final step.

In a small skillet over low heat, lightly toast almonds about 8 minutes, shaking pan occasionally.

Remove garlic skins. In food processor add the peeled garlic along with everything but the olive oil and cooking liquid. Turn the processor on and gradually add some of the cooking liquid. Keep adding the remainder of the water through the feed tube until the mixture is finely puréed. Add olive oil gradually, processing another 30 seconds. Refrigerate at least 2 hours before serving.

MAKES ABOUT 3 CUPS (700 ML)

Tuscan-style Bruschetta

¼ cup (60 mL) shallots, minced

2 Tbsp (30 mL) olive oil

3 cups (about 700 mL) Tuscan or other dark-leaved kale in chiffonade

2 Tbsp (30 mL) white wine

Black pepper to taste

3 Tbsp (45 mL) currants or coarsely chopped raisins

¼ cup (60 mL) pine nuts

½ cup (125 mL) grated Pecorino Romano

1 baguette

A little olive oil for brushing

An old *Gourmet* magazine was the inspiration for this, where kale now stands in for the spinach, and raisins or currants add subtle sweetness. You might want to pre-toast the pine nuts just a little. Serve plump fresh grapes in a bowl with the bruschetta along with a chunk of brie, Pecorino Romano or Fontina.

Preheat oven to 350F (175C).

In a medium skillet, cook the shallots in the olive oil 3 to 4 minutes until softened.

Add the kale and stir-fry about 5 minutes. Add wine and a little black pepper, and cover pan. Cook about 5 minutes until kale is tender. Remove from heat, add currants or raisins, pine nuts and grated Pecorino, stirring to combine.

Slice baguette thinly at an angle and brush lightly with olive oil. Toast in a 350F (175C) oven for 5 minutes or until golden. Spoon kale mixture onto baguette slices. If you like, serve them immediately or return bruschetta to the oven for another few minutes until filling is bubbly.

SERVES FOUR TO SIX

Ligurian Kale, Chard & Potato Torta

Crust:

1¼ cups (300 mL) unbleached white flour

½ tsp (2.5 mL) salt

½ tsp (2.5 mL) baking powder

2 Tbsp (30 mL) olive oil

1 Tbsp (15 mL) butter, softened

Cold water

Filling:

¾ cup (180 mL) mild feta, crumbled

¾ cup (180 mL) Jarlsberg or other mild soft cheese, grated

1 potato, boiled, peeled, chopped and cooled

1 small onion, minced

3 Tbsp (45 mL) parsley, minced

¼ tsp (1 mL) black pepper

2 cups (475 mL) kale leaves, loosely packed, cut in chiffonade

2 cups (475 mL) chard leaves, loosely packed, cut in chiffonade

Salt, to taste

2 eggs, lightly beaten

2 Tbsp (30 mL) olive oil, divided

Residents of the Liguria area of Italy still bake flattish pies like these over an open fire. Although it may seem as if there are a lot of steps, the result is eminently satisfying both for you and anyone else invited to share. Each step is easy, but make this when you have some time to spend in the kitchen. The crust is adaptable to other fillings, including fruit.

CRUST: Mix together dry ingredients, drizzle oil over top, add butter, then combine well with fork. Sprinkle water on a little at a time, adding up to a maximum of ½ cup (125 mL), to form a soft dough that just holds together. Knead the dough for about 30 seconds, then wrap and refrigerate for at least an hour. (You can make the crust in advance and store tightly wrapped in the refrigerator for up to a day.)

FILLING: Mix cheeses, potato, onion and parsley in a bowl, seasoning with pepper.

Cook the greens in a small amount of water until al dente. Drain in a colander, squeezing out as much liquid as you can into a bowl (again, save for soup, drink it or use in breakfast smoothies). Let stand 5 minutes, then try to squeeze out even more liquid. The last thing you need is a soggy torta.

Over

Continued from previous page.

Add greens to cheese/potato mixture. Depending on the saltiness of the feta cheese, it may be salty enough, but you can taste it now and add a pinch or two if you are so inclined.

Stir in eggs and 1 Tbsp (15 mL) olive oil.

Preheat oven to 375F (190C).

Remove dough from fridge and divide into two portions, one slightly bigger than the other. On a lightly floured surface, using a rolling pin, roll out larger ball to form a thin circle, approximately 13 inches (32 cm) in diameter, turning dough occasionally. It doesn't need to be perfectly round. In fact, it looks more rustic and authentic if it's a bit wonky.

Place the bottom crust on a cookie sheet covered with parchment paper. Gently pile filling on top, then use your hands or a flat spoon to evenly distribute it, leaving a 1-inch (2.5-cm) edge without any filling so that you can fold it in later.

Now, roll out the top crust (which will be a little smaller), and place it on top of the bottom crust and filling. Lightly moisten the bottom edge, then fold and crimp (pinch with your fingers) to seal. Pierce the surface here and there with a fork or knife tip to allow steam to escape.

Brush or drizzle torta with remaining olive oil. Bake until pale golden, about 30 to 35 minutes.

SERVES FOUR TO SIX

La Tarte with Kale, Olives & Gruyère

1 piece purchased puff pastry, thawed and rolled out thinly to about 9 by 13 inches (23 by 33 cm)

3 cups (700 mL) kale leaves in chiffonade

1 Tbsp (15 mL) olive oil

1 Tbsp (15 mL) butter

1 large onion, sliced thinly

2–3 cloves of garlic, crushed

⅓ cup (80 mL) pitted Moroccan olives, coarsely chopped

1 cup (250 mL) Gruyère or Emmental, coarsely grated

A riff on pissaladière (without the anchovies), this tarte features the strong, earthy flavour of Gruyère or Emmental—a lovely foil for the kale—while the olives add zing. Puff pastry is great to use every once in a while—it's easy to work with and the results are always appreciated. Look for decent puff pastry made with butter instead of lard or other fat. It's worth seeking out in the frozen-foods section.

This recipe lends itself to many tasty adaptations: feta and kalamata olives, for example.

Place puff pastry on a parchment-covered cookie sheet. Fold sides of pastry in slightly to form an edge. Set aside.

Steam kale for 3 or 4 minutes, then transfer to colander. Press out all the water you can. (Remember to put the colander over a bowl so you can collect the kale "juice" to use another time.)

Heat a large sauté pan over medium heat. Add the olive oil and butter, then sauté onion for about 5 minutes. Add well-drained kale and garlic and stir-fry another 5 minutes until kale is tender but not overcooked. Allow to cool about 5 minutes.

Preheat oven to 375F (190C) with oven rack in the middle. Arrange onion and kale mixture on top of puff pastry. Strew olive pieces around and sprinkle the cheese evenly over all. Bake about 20 minutes, or until lightly browned. Garnish with freshly chopped herbs—basil in summer, rosemary or sage in fall and winter.

SERVES SIX

Kale Edamame Fritters

1 cup (250 mL) frozen edamame

1 heaping cup (250 mL) kale leaves

½ tsp (2.5 mL) of salt, plus a
pinch or two

1 tsp (5 mL) ginger root, minced

½ tsp (2.5 mL) ground cumin

2 Tbsp (30 mL) water

2 eggs, separated

2 Tbsp (30 mL) flour

½ tsp (2.5 mL) baking powder

Vegetable oil for frying

Paper towels

My old-as-the-hills, falling-apart copy of *The Fanny Farmer Cookbook* inspired these fritters. The cover has been gone for years, and most of the index has disappeared but the all-important recipes remain. In any case, sometimes you just have to eat something fried, and while these aren't deep-fried like the corn fritters described in my tattered cookbook they nevertheless do the trick in a slightly healthier way. Don't skimp on the salt—trust me. Bet you can't eat just one. . .

Serve these fritters with Gorgeous Green Chutney (page 94) and sour cream.

In bowl of food processor, combine edamame, kale leaves, salt, ginger and cumin. Pulse briefly once or twice—the mixture should still be recognizable and not a paste. Add water, egg yolks, flour and baking powder—pulse once or twice more. Scrape mixture into a bowl.

Beat egg whites until they hold peaks but are not completely stiff. Using a spatula, fold into the edamame/kale mixture.

Heat a little oil in a large heavy-bottomed skillet on medium-high. Drop batter by spoonfuls and fry for about 3 minutes on each side. Turn the heat down a little once the fritters get frying. Do not crowd the fritters—fry 5 or 6 at a time, then remove and drain on paper towel. You'll have to add a little more oil to the pan each time. Serve with Gorgeous Green Chutney (page 94) and sour cream for dipping.

MAKES ABOUT TWENTY-FOUR 2-INCH (5-CM) FRITTERS

Gorgeous Green Chutney

1 cup (250 mL) cilantro, coarsely chopped

¼ cup (60 mL) chopped fresh mint leaves

1 tart apple (Granny Smith works well), cut into chunks

1 fresh jalapeño, seeded, deveined

1 medium tomato, cubed

2 tsp (10 mL) sugar

1 Tbsp (15 mL) lemon juice

1 small garlic clove, minced

½ tsp (2.5 mL) salt

½ tsp (2.5 mL) whole cumin seed

Thank you to Megan Hanna (no relation) for introducing me to this easy and unbelievably delicious "chutney." While it's actually more of a fresh salsa, regardless of the name, everyone who tastes it wants the recipe! Besides serving it along with the Kale Edamame Fritters, it's yummy with grilled chicken or fish, as a bruschetta topping, or on a crunchy rice cracker with a dab of goat's cheese, cream cheese or brie.

Whirl in a food processor briefly until ingredients are chopped fine, then serve.

MAKES ABOUT 1½ CUPS (375 ML)

Lavash "Pizza" with Kale, Mushrooms & Olives

 *

3 Tbsp (45 mL) olive oil, divided

1 large onion, halved, then thinly sliced

3 cloves garlic, minced

12–15 mushrooms (preferably brown), sliced thinly

2 tsp (10 mL) fresh rosemary leaves, minced finely

Salt and black pepper to taste

3 cups (700 mL) kale leaves

1 lavash (Middle Eastern bread)

Olive oil for brushing/drizzling

1 cup (250 mL) grated Asiago, Parmigiano-Reggiano, or Pecorino Romano, divided

½ cup (125 mL) pitted Moroccan or Lebanese olives, coarsely chopped

*if you omit the cheese

Middle Eastern flat bread is both convenient and quick—an alternative to making your own crust. If it's spring, you can add kale buds, too. To make this "pizza" more child-friendly, substitute mozzarella for the Parmigiano-Reggiano (or part of it).

Heat 2 Tbsp (30 mL) of the olive oil in a heavy skillet. Add the onions and sauté slowly until fragrant and softened—about 10 minutes. Add the garlic and sauté another 1–2 minutes.

Remove onion/garlic mixture from skillet into a bowl. Add 1 Tbsp (15 mL) olive oil to the pan, and fry the mushrooms until they begin to release their juices. Add the rosemary, sauté for a minute, then return onion/garlic mixture back into the skillet. Season with salt and pepper and set aside.

Lightly steam kale in a little water for 4 minutes until wilted. Remove, drain well and chop finely. Add to mixture in skillet.

Preheat oven to 350F (175C).

Place the lavash on a large baking sheet. (You might have to cut it a bit to make it fit, depending on the size of the pan.) Brush with olive oil, and sprinkle with one-third of the grated cheese.

Spoon greens mixture evenly atop lavash. Distribute olives on top, sprinkle on remaining cheese. With a light hand, drizzle a little more olive oil on top.

Bake about 12 minutes, or until lavash edges become crispy. Allow your pizza to rest for about 5 minutes, then serve. I like to use kitchen scissors to cut this pizza as I find they work better than a knife or pizza cutter.

SERVES TWO TO FOUR DEPENDING ON APPETITE

Kalekopita

10 cups (2.2 L) kale leaves—about
1 lb (454 gr)

2 Tbsp (30 mL) olive oil

1 large onion, minced

6 green onions including the green
parts, trimmed and chopped

¼ cup (60 mL) dried cranberries,
currants or apricots, chopped

¼ cup (60 mL) fresh mint leaves

2 tsp (10 mL) dried dillweed, or ¼
cup (60 mL) fresh if you have it

1½ cups (350 mL) feta
cheese, chopped

Pinch of black pepper

2 eggs, lightly beaten with a fork

½ cup (125 mL) olive oil combined
with ½ cup (125 mL) melted butter

12 filo sheets (about half a package)

Parchment paper

Dried fruit sweetens these Greek delicacies, guaranteed to convert anyone who is firmly "anti-kale." Sure, it's a bit of a project to make these luscious, buttery-crisp triangles, but well worth your time. Make an occasion of it: invite a few friends over, chat, sip tea or something stronger, and fold the filo. You will be a very popular guest if you bring these to a party or potluck. Make the kale filling a day or even two days ahead if you like.

Place kale in a large pot with lid, adding only a little water. Turn up the heat, put the lid on and steam for about 2 minutes or until kale is slightly wilted.

Drain kale in a colander, pressing out as much liquid as you can into a bowl to freeze for future use in soup, etc. When the kale is cool enough to be handled, squeeze it to remove more liquid. (It's important that the kale not be soppy.) Chop kale finely.

Heat olive oil in a skillet, and sauté onions over low heat until slightly soft, about 5 minutes. Add the green onions and sauté a few more minutes.

Transfer the onion mixture to a medium bowl. Add the chopped kale, dried fruit, mint leaves, dill, feta and pepper. Combine lightly, then allow the mixture to sit and cool slightly. Lightly mix in the beaten eggs.

You're now ready to roll—or should I say, fold!

Lay down one sheet of filo, short side toward you.

Brush the bottom half of the sheet sparingly with butter mixture.

Fold in half, toward you, to form a rectangle.

Over

More than a word about filo

Because it is super thin, filo (or phyllo) dries out very quickly when exposed to air, so using these tips will help to make your experience successful.

1. Organize your supplies and have everything you need within reach: the filling, the oil/butter mixture, your pastry brush and a blade or sharp knife.

2. Always cover the filo, once out of its packaging, with a plastic bag. Place a well-wrung damp dishtowel on top of the plastic bag. (You can't put the damp towel directly on the filo sheets because they will disintegrate.)

3. Unroll 4 sheets (enough for 8 triangles) at a time from the packaging, then gently fold each in half and place inside a plastic bag. Remove a sheet at a time, placing it on a pliable plastic "chopping board" or surface.

At this point you are probably thinking you'd just rather take a run down to the deli and buy your appetizer. Hang in there and in no time you'll be opening your own Greek bakery.

Continued from previous page.

Turn the rectangle so that the short side is again toward you.

Using a knife or sharp blade, cut the folded filo in half, lengthwise. You now have two long strips of double filo. Start with the first and put a spoonful of filling on the bottom left corner. Brush the rest of the strip lightly with the butter mixture.

Fold the lower right-hand corner of the filo towards the other edge to form a triangle. Don't worry if a bit of filling comes out— by the time you turn the sheet a few times it will be fully encased.

As if you were folding a flag, keep forming triangles.

Eventually the triangle-making stops at the top. Brush the top lightly with the butter mixture. If there's a bit of an uneven edge, fold that over. The butter will keep it in place.

I usually freeze at least half of the triangles before baking on a parchment-lined baking sheet. When they're frozen, they are transferred to a freezer bag for storage.

To bake your kalekopita triangles, preheat the oven to 350F (175C). Place the triangles on cookie sheets lined with parchment paper and bake for 15 to 20 minutes, or until nicely browned.

MAKES ABOUT TWENTY-FOUR 4-INCH (10-CM) TRIANGLES

SALADS

The Queen of Greens

Ironically, many of us were first exposed to the healthiest green on the planet in the form of a garnish—a curly leaf of kale at the side of a plate, seldom eaten. But the Queen of Greens is having her come-uppance, rising to the top of the charts!

Kale is now causing a commotion in restaurants and showing up on more kitchen tables, and that's a good thing. One cup of raw kale gives you more vitamins and super nutrients than you can shake a stick at—and with so many delicious ways to enjoy it you'll want to eat it every day!

While kale is available all year in stores it can also be grown year round in your very own garden. Kale is a real blessing in winter to gardeners, as January and February are fairly dreary, both greens-wise and garden-wise. Amazingly, a cold snap actually makes kale taste sweeter.

Some salad-y ideas

· Add chopped or thinly sliced kale to any favourite salad or coleslaw.

· Pair kale with slices of peeled oranges, chopped pitted prunes, grated cheese, green olives, fresh dates or juicy halved cherries in summer.

· Go nuts—add a few almonds, cashews, walnuts, filberts or pecans to some thinly sliced or shredded kale. A dash of olive oil and a drizzle of lemon, lime or orange juice is enough adornment. Or for a super treat, add a little bit of goat's cheese.

· Line a plate with kale chiffonade, then add drained canned chickpeas, good canned tuna, steamed green beans, cucumber and a few olives. Dress lightly, et voilà: Niçoise-ish salad.

· Perfect little leaves of flat-leafed kale ('Lacinato', 'Rainbow Tuscan', or the Portuguese variety) on crudité platters are yummy and handy for scooping up dips.

· Kale stands in for lettuce in wraps filled with spicy ground pork with hoisin sauce, or the ubiquitous Thai condiment called Sweet Chili Sauce for Chicken.

· Your favourite potato salad benefits from the nutritional oomph of added finely chopped curly kale.

· Keep a container or bag of washed kale leaves for last-minute use in sandwiches. Teach your kids and teens to think of using it just like lettuce.

· Use small kale leaves to make "ears" that you can stick into baked potatoes for a fun meal for children.

A word on the texture of kale leaves in salads

One of the great things about kale's thick leaves is their resistance to pests and other environmental stressors. Kale also has the ability to withstand super-cold temperatures. When you wash kale, you will notice how it resists water. This impermeability means that salad dressings may not adhere or penetrate the leaves in the way to which you are accustomed. (One great feature of kale, in fact, is that it has more staying power than lettuce and resists getting soggy. Not to mention it has tons more nutrition and flavour!) In any case, in order to enjoy kale raw, many people prefer the leaves softened slightly. There are a few ways to do this: rub or massage the kale a little (we can all use a little massage) in order to break down the cells, cut in chiffonade, or let the salad rest a little while in the dressing.

Teen Apple Kale Toss

2–3 handfuls of kale

One cored and grated or chopped apple

This recipe was developed by my friend Heather's son, Callum Glass. At Heather's house, they had to compete with the chickens for the kale so eventually they built a hen house with a fence. Before that, whenever the kale began to grow, the chickens quickly mowed it down!

I'd drizzle on a little honey-sweetened vinaigrette but Callum likes it plain.

Combine 2 to 3 handfuls of finely chopped kale per person with grated or chopped apple. Serve. That's it.

SERVES ONE HUNGRY TEENAGER

Garlicky Kale with Walnuts

  *

8 cups (2 L) kale leaves

½ cup (125 mL) walnut pieces

3 large cloves garlic

A pinch of salt

Juice of 1 lemon

Olive oil (optional)

Asiago or Pecorino Romano cheese
in thin shards (optional)

*if you skip the cheese

An Italian mezzaluna works well to chop this rudimentary salad that can also be served as an appetizer, piled onto pita or crackers, or rolled in a wrap. Otherwise, just use your trusty sharp chef's knife. Without the optional oil and/or cheese, it's a cleansing tonic salad, easily made in two minutes flat.

Place kale, walnuts and garlic on a board, and using a mezzaluna or sharp knife, chop everything together until fine. Pile into a bowl and dress with the salt and lemon juice. Add olive oil and cheese if desired.

SERVES FOUR

Kale Gomae

4 Tbsp (60 mL) sesame seeds

1 Tbsp (15 mL) mirin

1 Tbsp (15 mL) light Japanese soy
sauce or regular tamari

4 cups (1 L) tightly packed young
kale leaves

*with non-gluten soy sauce

My friend Wendy MacDonald consulted with her Japanese sewing-class friends to learn just exactly what is in gomae dressing. Lo and behold, there are only three ingredients. This is just like the dish you would be served in a Japanese restaurant—but made with kale instead of spinach.

A suribachi is a low ceramic grinding bowl etched with grooves that comes with a wooden implement called a surikogi. It has a rounded end, and is very useful for grinding spices and other things like ginger and garlic for curry paste.

Toast sesame seeds by shaking them in a small cast-iron or other heavy-bottomed pan over medium-low heat. It won't take long so don't leave the stove; keep shaking until the seeds become lightly fragrant and slightly darkened, but not browned.

In a suribachi or mortar and pestle (or food processor, but the suribachi is much groovier!), grind the toasted sesame seeds, mirin and soy until a kind of thin paste results.

Lightly steam the kale for about 1 minute in very little water. Drain thoroughly, squeezing all the liquid out. On each small plate, place one-quarter of the kale leaves, squeezed together tightly into the traditional boxy gomae shape, or make little mounds. Drizzle the dressing on the kale with a little extra around the plate, and eat your Kale Gomae with chopsticks.

SERVES FOUR

Kale-Dorf Salad

 *

4 cups (1 L) kale leaves in chiffonade

1 cup (250 mL) tart apple (unpeeled), chopped

2 Tbsp (30 mL) dried cranberries, chopped

1 cup (250 mL) celery, sliced thin

¼ cup (60 mL) walnuts, lightly toasted and chopped

¼ cup (60 mL) fresh dates, chopped fine

Dressing:

1 tsp (5 mL) sugar

1 Tbsp (15 mL) lemon juice

1 Tbsp (15 mL) white wine vinegar

2 Tbsp (30 mL) olive oil

Pinch of black pepper

2 Tbsp (30 mL) mayonnaise

*if egg-free mayonnaise is used

I like the crunch of curly kale in this takeoff on Waldorf salad, originally created in New York's Waldorf Hotel in the late 1800s.

Toss kale, chopped apples, cranberries, celery, walnuts and dates in a salad or serving bowl. In a small bowl, whisk the dressing ingredients well, then pour over the salad, mixing well. Allow your Kale-Dorf Salad to sit for 5 minutes or so before serving to allow the kale to relax.

SERVES TWO GENEROUSLY

Tabouli with Quinoa & Kale

2 cups (475 mL) water

1 cup (250 mL) quinoa

1 cup (250 mL) kale leaves, minced or finely chopped (retain stems for stock)

1 cup (250 mL) parsley, minced or finely chopped (retain stems for stock)

2 large cloves garlic, finely minced

1 cup (250 mL) scallions, chopped

¼ cup (60 mL) lemon juice

¼ cup (60 mL) olive oil

2 Tbsp (30 mL) fresh mint, chopped, or 2 tsp (10 mL) dried mint, crushed (optional)

Salt and black pepper

2 large ripe tomatoes, chopped

This is a very pretty green and red salad that works as a main course, salad or wrap filling. Or, you can really "go green" and use it as a dip for larger leaves from the garden—lettuce, or tender baby kale leaves. This tabouli really needs to be made a couple of hours ahead so that the flavours can mellow and meld. It keeps well for several days in the fridge. Refrigeration doesn't do tomatoes any favour, so add them just before serving.

To make a simple vegetable stock, toss saved kale and parsley stems into water and bring to a boil, then simmer uncovered for a few minutes. Strain out solids.

Add the quinoa to vegetable stock. Bring to a gentle boil, then let simmer for about 15 minutes. Allow to cool and toss with the remaining ingredients except tomatoes, adding salt and pepper to taste.

Refrigerate for at least 2 hours and add tomatoes just before serving.

SERVES FOUR GENEROUSLY

Kale Caesar!

VG* GF*

1 clove garlic, bruised with a heavy knife

2 Tbsp (30 mL) olive oil

2 thick slices dense country-style bread

2 medium (not hard) boiled eggs

2 large cloves garlic

5 anchovy filets (more or less, as you like)

¼ cup (60 mL) lemon juice

1 Tbsp (15 mL) balsamic vinegar

1 tsp (5 mL) Worcestershire sauce

Black pepper

½ cup (125 mL) plus 2 Tbsp (30 mL) olive oil

8 cups (2 L) kale leaves, freshly washed (about 1 lb)

½ cup (125 mL) grated Parmigiano-Reggiano

2 Tbsp (30 mL) capers, drained

*gluten-free with non-gluten bread; vegetarian without Worcestershire sauce and anchovies

Tuscan kale might seem appropriate for this tangy, toothsome offering, but curly kale is crunchier, so I prefer to use it. If you are easing your family into the idea of raw kale, use part romaine lettuce the first time or two.

Make croutons: rub the inside of a small bowl all over with the garlic. Add the olive oil and stir with a wooden spoon. Trim crusts from bread and cut into 1-inch (2.5-cm) chunks. Toss croutons in the bowl until well coated.

Heat a non-stick skillet, add the croutons and sauté, tossing frequently until they brown lightly.

Shell the cooked eggs and chop whites finely or put them through a sieve. Set aside.

In a blender, process the egg yolks, garlic, anchovies, lemon juice, balsamic vinegar, Worcestershire and generous grindings of pepper. Add olive oil a little at a time so the mixture becomes emulsified.

Cut or tear kale into bite-sized pieces. Transfer kale to a clean cotton towel, wrapping lightly to dry. Add kale to the salad bowl. Toss with dressing to coat all the leaves, add the cheese, capers and croutons, toss lightly and sprinkle with reserved egg whites.

SERVES FOUR

Tuscan Kale with White Beans & Roasted Garlic

8 cups (2 L) Tuscan kale, trimmed and cut in chiffonade

1½ cups (350 mL) cooked cannellini or other white beans, drained

3 whole heads of garlic, roasted, cloves removed and skinned

6–8 beautiful red radishes, quartered

6 small tomatoes, quartered

Flat Italian parsley leaves, for garnish

This super-easy composed salad is great for a potluck or weekend lunch. If you want more protein, quartered hard-boiled eggs would fit well on the platter.

Place chiffonade on a platter or in shallow, wide bowl. Scatter beans around artfully, then compose the salad by placing the veggies all over. Garnish with parsley.

Dress with one of the basil vinaigrettes (recipes follow) or another that you like.

SERVES FOUR TO SIX

Basil Vinaigrette

3 Tbsp (45 mL) wine vinegar

1 clove garlic

¼ cup (60 mL) olive oil

1 Tbsp (15 mL) honey

1 tsp (5 mL) Dijon mustard

Pinch of salt

¼ cup (60 mL) fresh basil leaves

Odessa Bromley, garden designer and friend, gave me the recipe for this fragrant, creamy basil vinaigrette. Odessa and her husband, Dave, are major volunteers at the Sunshine Coast Botanical Garden on Mason Road in Sechelt, BC, and also operate Rose Lane B&B in beautiful Roberts Creek.

In a blender, process until creamy, adding a bit of extra oil if needed.

MAKES ABOUT ¾ CUP (180 ML)

〜〜〜〜〜〜〜〜〜〜〜〜〜〜〜〜〜〜〜

West Creek Farm Vinaigrette

½ small red onion, sliced

1 tsp (5 mL) chopped garlic

1 tsp (5 mL) sugar

1 tsp (5 mL) salt

⅓ cup (80 mL) balsamic vinegar

¼ cup (60 mL) basil leaves

⅔ cup (160 mL) olive oil

This creation of chef Nathan Hyam was featured at a West Creek Farm party a few years back, and it was a big hit. West Creek is a soil-manufacturing company in Fort Langley, the birthplace of BC. They make very good soil that grows great kale!

Enjoy this dressing on raw kale or raw anything—cooked or grilled veggies, too.

Purée everything in a blender. To vary, add finely minced rosemary, lavender and thyme —but just a tiny bit.

MAKES ABOUT 1½ CUPS (375 ML)

Kale Serenade on a Mandoline

4 cups (1 L) kale leaves, packed

2 cups (475 mL) sui choi

1 cup (250 mL) red cabbage

1 cup (250 mL) carrots

1 orange or red bell pepper

½ cup (125 mL) parsley, minced
(don't use the mandoline)

Dressing:

2 tsp (10 mL) sesame oil

3 Tbsp (45 mL) vegetable oil

2 tsp (10 mL) tamari or soy sauce

1 clove garlic, minced

1 tsp (5 mL) ginger root,
finely minced

2 Tbsp (30 mL) rice vinegar

Salt and black pepper

*if non-gluten soy sauce is used

A different kind of music is made with this kind of mandoline, from the recipe collection of Barb Coward. Barb had raised beds built in her lane on the west side of Vancouver, where she grows giant vegetables including monster zucchini plants and corn as high as an elephant's eye.

Using a mandoline (carefully—they are very sharp!) makes salad-making a joy and a snap. You can add beets as well but put them on the top last, otherwise the salad will be bright pink.

Cut the kale leaves using the chiffonade method and transfer to a serving bowl. Using a mandoline or sharp knife, cut the sui choi, red cabbage, carrots and bell pepper into very thin shreds. Add all the veggies to the kale, and toss lightly.

In a small bowl, whisk together the dressing ingredients briskly. Pour over the salad and combine well, then refrigerate for 15 minutes before serving.

SERVES SIX

Lightly Massaged Kale with Alligator Pear

8 cups (2 L) Tuscan kale leaves in chiffonade

½ tsp (2.5 mL) salt

1 large sweet red bell pepper

3 Tbsp (45 mL) currants

1 perfectly ripe large avocado or two small ones, diced

¼ cup (60 mL) pine nuts, lightly toasted

Vinaigrette:

1 Tbsp (15 mL) lime juice

1 Tbsp (15 mL) white wine vinegar

¼ cup (60 mL) olive oil

2 tsp (10 mL) shallots, finely minced

Black pepper

Did you know that avocados used to be called "alligator pears"? One of my oldest memories is of my parents stopping their car on the highway somewhere in California because there were avocados all over the side of the road. At the age of five, I was unimpressed, but my parents were thrilled—clearly, these bumpy-skinned green fruits were a delicacy to them.

Place kale chiffonade in a serving bowl. Rub the salt into the kale with your hands, massaging it lightly for a few minutes or until you can feel it relax a little. Quarter the red pepper, removing the white parts, and slice thinly. Add the red pepper slices and currants to the kale.

Prepare the vinaigrette: In a small bowl, whisk the lime juice, vinegar, olive oil and shallots with a little pepper. Pour over the salad and add the diced avocado, tossing gently. Sprinkle with pine nuts, then dive in.

SERVES FOUR

Creamy Tahini Kale with Pomegranate & Lime

8 cups (2 L) kale leaves in chiffonade

½ tsp (2.5 mL) salt

¼ cup (60 mL) red onion, finely chopped

½ cup cucumber, chopped

1 red bell pepper, seeded, deveined and chopped

¼ cup (60 mL) fresh dates, seeded and chopped

½ cup (125 mL) pomegranate seeds or more

Tahini Dressing:

½ cup (125 mL) tahini

2 garlic cloves, coarsely chopped

2 Tbsp (30 mL) lime juice

1 tsp (5 mL) lime zest

1 Tbsp (15 mL) nutritional yeast

¼ cup (60 mL) olive oil

½ tsp (2.5 mL) salt

Black pepper to taste

⅓ cup (80 mL) water

This is a super-satisfying winter salad. Pomegranates are readily available in the colder months, adding their crunch and stained-glass colour. Since the tahini vinaigrette is somewhat elaborate, the recipe makes enough for a few salads. It's also delicious on brown rice, and keeps well in the fridge for a week or more.

Mix kale and salt in a large salad bowl. Lightly massage the kale for a few minutes. Add the onion, cucumber, bell pepper and dates; toss lightly.

Process the vinaigrette ingredients in a blender until smooth and creamy.

Drizzle some of the tahini dressing on the salad and toss lightly. Sprinkle the pomegranate seeds over top before serving. Pass around extra vinaigrette if desired.

SERVES FOUR

Wilted Kale with Pickled Red Onions

 *

1 heaping Tbsp (15 mL) brown sugar

2 Tbsp (30 mL) balsamic vinegar

½ cup (125 mL) water

½ cup (125 mL) red onion, thinly sliced

2 thin slices of pancetta or good-quality smoky bacon (optional)

1 tsp (5 mL) vegetable or olive oil

2 Tbsp (30 mL) finely minced shallots

8 or 10 smallish sage leaves in chiffonade

4 big handfuls of small kale leaves—about 4 cups (1 L) packed

¼ cup (60 mL) Asiago, Parmigiano-Reggiano or Romano, grated

Black pepper

*if served without the pancetta

Another winter offering, this one redolent with sage. I recommend it as an excellent pick-me-up after overindulgence around the winter holiday season. Feel free to omit the pancetta or bacon—the salad is almost as good without it.

In a small saucepan bring the brown sugar, vinegar and water to a boil. Add the red onions, then lower heat to simmer and cook for about 10 minutes. Let the onions "pickle" in the pot for at least 30 minutes; the mixture will be slightly thickened.

Dice the pancetta or bacon, then sauté in the oil in a large skillet over medium-low heat for about 3 minutes. Add the shallots and sauté until shallots are soft and meat is browned, about 5 minutes. Add the sage, stir and cook for a minute, then add the kale and sauté for 2 minutes until kale wilts. Transfer kale mixture to a serving bowl. Toss with the onions, their pickled liquid and the cheese. Add a few grindings of pepper, and enjoy the salad warm.

SERVES TWO

Kale Salad with Pears, Pecans & Blue Cheese

1 large, firm, almost ripe pear (about 8 oz or 225 gr)

2 Tbsp (30 mL) butter

Dash of cinnamon

½ cup (125 mL) pecans

Black pepper

At least 8 cups (2 L) kale leaves, coarsely chopped—more is okay

2 oz (50 gr) blue cheese, in bits

Vinaigrette:

2 Tbsp (30 mL) white wine vinegar

¼ cup (60 mL) olive oil

1 tsp (5 mL) grainy mustard

1 small garlic clove, minced

¼ tsp (1 mL) salt

The sweetness of pear, the crunch of pecans, and—if you like—the rich bite of aged cheese—aaaaahhh. What a way to complement kale! Really, you can use any kind of blue cheese—Stilton, Roquefort, Gorgonzola, Cambozola—and very little goes a long way. If you aren't a strong-cheese fan, use mild soft goat's cheese instead, or simply omit the cheese.

Halve the pear, remove the core, and slice thinly, creating about 12 slices. In a medium-sized skillet over low heat, melt the butter. Add the pear pieces, sprinkle with cinnamon and sauté about 10 minutes, shaking the pan occasionally, until pears are somewhat caramelized and softened. Set pan aside.

In a small cast-iron skillet or other small pan, toast the pecans over medium-low heat, stirring and shaking the pan often, until slightly browned and aromatic—about 8 minutes. Remove pecans from heat and chop them coarsely.

Whisk the vinaigrette ingredients in a small bowl. Place the kale on a platter. Carefully transfer the pears, strew the pecans and drizzle the vinaigrette over the kale. Dot cheese over top, or garnish individual plates with the cheese.

SERVES FOUR

SOUPS & STEWS

Garlicky Kale & Asian Greens with Chicken

6 cups (1.4 L) chicken stock, preferably homemade

6 large cloves (or more) garlic, peeled

4 cups (1 L) kale leaves in chiffonade

2 cups (475 mL) coarsely chopped bok choy, sui choy, or other Asian greens

3 Tbsp (45 mL) olive oil

2 tsp (10 mL) ground cumin

1 tsp (5 mL) ground coriander

½ tsp (2.5 mL) ground turmeric

2 Tbsp (30 mL) fresh ginger root, minced

1 tsp (5 mL) brown sugar

Juice of 1 lemon, plus 4 lemon slices

Salt and black pepper to taste

About 2 cups (475 mL) cooked chicken, torn in bite-sized pieces

Lots of jasmine rice, cooked

Cilantro or parsley leaves to garnish

A great way to make use of leftover chicken—even takeout. My youngest son, Ted, gets into doing chicken with rice the way it's served in Thailand each time he returns from diving sojourns. This is Ted's soup style, but with a few more ingredients; a fragrant heart-warmer, it packs a wallop of garlic, greens and spices to knock a cold or flu into next week. If you've saved some kale stock, use some in place of the chicken stock to add even more vitamins and minerals.

Bring stock to a relaxed boil in a medium saucepan. If you have a bamboo skewer, skewer 3 garlic cloves and cook in the stock for 5 minutes. Remove skewer, mash garlic, set aside. (If you don't have a skewer, just toss them in and after five minutes, remove them.)

Add the kale and greens and reduce heat to medium-low. Simmer, allowing greens to wilt slightly—about 5 minutes. Add braised mashed garlic into broth/greens mixture.

Heat oil in a small skillet over medium heat. Add cumin, coriander and turmeric and stir until spices release their fragrance—a few minutes. Thinly slice then add the other 3 garlic cloves and ginger root. Cook and stir another 2 to 3 minutes, stirring in the brown sugar.

Meanwhile, add lemon juice to broth and greens, and season lightly with salt and pepper. Add the sautéed spice mixture, using a little of the soup to deglaze the small skillet. Simmer over very low heat for about 10 more minutes and stir in chopped chicken to heat through.

Evenly divide the cooked rice among 4 large bowls. Ladle soup over the rice, then garnish with cilantro leaves and the lemon slices.

SERVES FOUR GENEROUSLY

Mother of Invention Soup with Kale

*

2 tsp (10 mL) vegetable oil

1 small onion, chopped

3 cloves garlic, minced

1 walnut-sized piece of fresh ginger, minced

2 cups (475 mL) kale in chiffonade

1 cup (250 mL) kale buds (or broccoli florets including peeled stems), coarsely chopped

1 cup (250 mL) cabbage, chopped

1 cup (250 mL) or so of canned tomatoes, coarsely chopped

4 cups (1 L) chicken broth (and/or kale or other vegetable broth)

Salt and black pepper

Soba (buckwheat) noodles—I used one paper-wrapped "group," about 4 oz (100 gr), but you could use more, or less.

*if vegetable stock is used

Not Frank Zappa, but using up what was in the fridge—three members of the *Brassica* family, leftover canned tomatoes and excellent chicken/potato/kale broth. It was ready to eat in 30 minutes! Buckwheat noodles make the soup extra nourishing—it's a good source of tryptophan as well as all other essential amino acids. Look for 100 percent buckwheat noodles—they do exist, though sometimes you have to search a little. Buckwheat is not a grain—it's the seed part of a plant related to rhubarb and sorrel, and it's gluten-free in addition to being high in protein.

In a medium to large saucepan over medium heat, cook the onion, garlic and ginger in the vegetable oil for about 5 minutes. Add the kale, broccoli and cabbage and cook, stirring, until the vegetables are coated with the onions and seasonings. Add the tomatoes and broth. Bring to a boil, then lower heat and simmer about 20 minutes.

Meanwhile, bring another pot of water to a boil. Add noodles and cook according to package directions—usually about 5 minutes. Drain and add to soup, seasoning with salt and pepper if desired.

SERVES TWO TO THREE

Soothing Miso with Kale for One

 *

1 Tbsp (15 mL) miso paste

1 Tbsp (15 mL) water

1 minced garlic clove

2 tsp (10 mL) minced fresh ginger root (or to taste)

2 oz (about 60 gr) soba noodles—preferably 100 percent buckwheat

2 cups (475 mL) water

1 cup (250 mL) very fresh kale leaves in chiffonade

1 small carrot, in matchstick pieces

1 small piece of daikon, in matchstick pieces

2 oz (about 60 gr) tofu ("firm, not extra firm," Gail says)

2 tsp (10 mL) soy sauce or tamari

Dash of organic sesame oil

*if non-gluten miso paste and buckwheat noodles are used

Another recipe from my dear friend Gail, this concoction is eminently satisfying, and so. . . clean, even more so if you run out to the garden to pick the kale just before putting it in the soup. Buckwheat and kale are a match made in heaven—both seem perfect foods for winter.

Double or triple the recipe if you like. If you have a mandoline, use it to cut the veggies into matchsticks.

Put the miso in a beautiful (preferably pottery) bowl large enough to hold about 3 cups (700 mL) of liquid. Add the water, garlic and ginger, and stir well.

Cook the soba according to package directions until al dente. Drain and add to the bowl.

Bring 2 cups (475 mL) water to a boil in a small pot. Add the kale, matchstick veggies and tofu. Cook about 2 minutes. Pour the contents of the pot into the serving bowl, along with as much of the cooking water as you can. Add the soy and sesame oil. Gently swirl everything with chopsticks or a spoon, then enjoy!

MAKES ONE GENEROUS BOWL OF SOUP

Kale Borscht with Vodka & Fresh Mint

1 Tbsp (15 mL) olive oil

1 Tbsp (15 mL) butter

1 small tender fennel bulb—about 1 cup (250 mL) coarsely chopped

1 medium onion, chopped

2 big cloves of garlic, minced

¼ tsp (1 mL) chili flakes or to taste

2 medium beets, scrubbed and chopped

1 waxy potato, such as 'Yukon Gold', peeled and chopped

Scant ¼ cup (60 mL) loosely packed fresh mint leaves, chopped

5 cups (1.2 L) vegetable or chicken stock

1 Tbsp (15 mL) balsamic vinegar

2 cups (475 mL) Tuscan kale in very fine chiffonade

½ cup (125 mL) vodka

Tiny kale leaves for garnish

*vegetarian if vegetable stock is used; vegan if vegetable stock is used and olive oil is used instead of butter

This suave (and very grown-up) soup would be perfect for a fancy dinner party. Pair with rosemary olive-oil bread, as well as cold vodka shooters if you are so inclined.

In a large heavy-bottomed pot, sauté the fennel, onion, garlic and chili flakes in the oil and butter for about 5 minutes, stirring frequently.

Add the beets and potatoes and stir-fry over medium-low another 5 minutes. Add mint leaves and stock; simmer for 15 to 20 minutes or until potatoes and beets are tender.

Using an immersion blender or food processor, blend the soup with the balsamic vinegar. Return soup to pot. Add the super-thin kale chiffonade and simmer for 5 minutes or until kale is tender but still bright green. Add vodka.

Serve in fancy bowls with a dollop of crème fraiche or sour cream, and garnish with 1 or 2 small kale leaves.

SERVES FOUR TO SIX AS A STARTER OR AMUSE-BOUCHE

Doukhobor Kale & Beet Borscht

2 Tbsp (30 mL) vegetable oil

1 large onion, chopped

3 garlic cloves, minced

½ tsp (2.5 mL) cumin seed

2 tsp (10 mL) dried dillweed

3 cups (700 mL) cabbage in chiffonade

4 cups (1 L) kale leaves in chiffonade

2 potatoes, peeled and grated

1 parsnip, peeled and grated

6 cups (1.4 L) vegetable stock or water

About ½ lb (225 gr) beets, scrubbed and grated

2 Tbsp (30 mL) ketchup

2 Tbsp (30 mL) balsamic vinegar

1 Tbsp (15 mL) honey

Salt and black pepper

1 cup (250 mL) peas, fresh or frozen

½ cup (125 mL) parsley leaves, minced

Sour cream or yogurt for serving (optional)

*vegan when served without the sour cream or yogurt (or using a vegan-friendly sour cream substitute); gluten-free if non-gluten ketchup is used

The best borscht memory I have was from a hotel in Grand Forks, BC. It included peas that seemed as if they'd been recently shelled, and was a little creamy—the cook might have even added cream or milk. We ate it in front of a large window overlooking the surrounding fields.

I have no idea if Doukhobors put kale in their borscht but if they don't, they should, as it makes it even higher in protective phytonutrients. It seems to taste better if made at least half a day before you eat it, or even the day before.

In a large heavy-bottomed pot, heat oil over medium-low. Add onion and stir-fry about 3 minutes until onion softens. Add the garlic and cumin, and cook another few minutes.

Add the dillweed, cabbage, kale, potato and parsnip. Cook and stir for 2 minutes, then add the stock, grated beets, ketchup, balsamic and honey. Bring to a boil, then lower heat and simmer, covered, about 20 minutes. Taste, adding salt and pepper if you like. Add the peas and parsley. Simmer another 8 to 10 minutes, adding water if necessary, until veggies are tender. When serving, add a spoonful of sour cream or yogurt, if you like.

SERVES SIX

Cornmeal Dumplings

⅔ cup (160 mL) cornmeal
⅔ cup (160 mL) unbleached flour
½ tsp (2.5 mL) baking soda
¼ tsp (1 mL) baking powder
½ tsp (2.5 mL) salt
2 tsp (10 mL) sugar
1 egg
1 cup (250 mL) buttermilk
2 Tbsp (30 mL) butter, melted

Combine dry ingredients in medium bowl. Beat the egg and buttermilk in a small bowl and add the melted butter.

Make a well in the centre of the dry ingredients, then add the liquid mixture, stirring only to combine. The dumpling batter should be a little like a stiff cake batter. If it's too dry, add a little more buttermilk but do not overmix.

Cook per directions in Autumn Kale Stew (page 125).

SERVES FOUR GENEROUSLY

Karefree Kale & Spud Soup with Italian Sausage

1 Tbsp (15 mL) olive oil

1 cup (250 mL) chopped onion

1 cup (250 mL) chopped carrot

2 cloves garlic, crushed

1 bay leaf

½ lb (225 gr) mild Italian sausage, casings removed, cut in 1-inch (2.5-cm) pieces

2 potatoes, peeled and cubed or sliced

4 cups (1 L) water or stock

3 cups (700 mL) kale leaves, chopped

Salt and black pepper

Lemon juice

Chopped parsley

*if gluten-free sausage is used

This was another soup whipped up with "what was in the fridge" along with what was growing in the garden in December—kale! There was a little bedraggled parsley that made it into the soup as well. Because it's relatively simple, most kids won't have a problem with it; if you want to add more kale, go ahead and make it more stew-y.

In a medium saucepan fitted with a lid, sauté the onions and carrots in the olive oil over medium heat for about 5 minutes, stirring, or until onions are translucent. Add the crushed garlic and bay leaf; continue to sauté a few more minutes.

Add sausage, breaking up with a fork. Sauté until meat is no longer pink—5 or 6 minutes. Add potatoes and sauté 5 more minutes, stirring, then add stock or water. Allow soup to bubble over low heat about 15 minutes or until potatoes are almost tender. Add the kale and salt and pepper to taste, and simmer for about 5 minutes. If the soup seems too thick, add more stock or water.

Garnish with fresh lemon juice and chopped parsley before serving. A dash of good olive oil is great too. Like many soups, this one improves if made a day ahead.

SERVES FOUR

Hearty Kale & Red Pepper Chowder

4 Tbsp (60 mL) butter

1½ cups (350 mL) onion, chopped

2 large red bell peppers, seeded and thinly sliced

4 cups (1 L) kale, chopped

6 cups (1.4 L) chicken or vegetable broth

4 large 'Yukon Gold' potatoes, peeled, cut into 1-inch (2.5-cm) chunks

2 Tbsp (30 mL) cornstarch

2 Tbsp (30 mL) water

1 cup (250 mL) sour cream

18 oz (500 gr) firm boneless white fish cut in bite-sized pieces

¼ cup (60 mL) parsley leaves, minced, plus extra for garnish

Salt and black pepper

Lemon wedges

Once upon a time, I was married to a member of a band known as "Papa Bear's Medicine Show" and Papa Bear's wife, George (short for Georgina), made this soup. George and Papa Bear lived in Richmond then, in a tiny house with a woodstove and a yard completely filled with daffodils in spring.

George was American and had gotten the recipe from a *Sunset* magazine circa 1972. This was a special made-for-company dish because of the fish and the sour cream; we were all quite poor then. The addition of kale adds an array of vitamins and phytonutrients to the chowder. Enjoy it with dense, crusty bread.

Melt butter in a heavy-bottomed soup pot over medium heat. Add the onions and cook, stirring frequently, until they soften slightly—about 5 minutes. Add the red peppers and kale. Continue to cook, stirring frequently for 5 minutes more.

Add broth and potatoes. Increase heat, bringing the mixture to a boil. Reduce heat and simmer until potatoes are al dente—about 8 minutes.

In a small bowl, mix together the cornstarch, water and sour cream. To prevent curdling, ladle a little of the hot broth into the cornstarch mixture, stir well, and add it back to the soup. Cook over low heat, stirring, until the soup thickens slightly. Add the fish and parsley, and simmer over low heat (barely bubbling) until the fish is cooked to your liking—don't overcook as the fish will keep cooking after you remove the chowder from the heat. Taste, adding salt and pepper if desired.

Garnish with parsley, and serve with lemon wedges.

SERVES FOUR AS A MAIN COURSE

Oma's Pea Soup with Kale & Celeriac

1 cup (250 mL) dried yellow peas

6 cups (1.4 L) water

1 bay leaf

1 tsp (5 mL) zout (salt)

1 medium onion, chopped

1 small celeriac root, trimmed and chopped

2 carrots, peeled and chopped

1 large potato or about 1 cup (250 mL) leftover mashed potatoes

2 cups (475 mL) kale leaves, tightly packed, in chiffonade

½ cup (125 mL) parsley, minced, plus more for garnish

Salt and black pepper

Another easy (and Dutch) rendition. The Oma referred to here is my son Jesse's grandmother and my mother-in-law who lived to be almost 98. Oma ("grandma" in Dutch) was both an opera singer and voice teacher who immigrated to Canada in the 1950s. Marguerite Bradbury, also an Oma, is a friend and colleague who helped me with the Dutch names—*Erwtensoep* and *zout*—both lose in the translation! This is plain comfort food, and excellent for using up leftover mashed potatoes if you were bad and didn't eat all your "Stampot" (see page 180).

Rinse the peas, then put them in a covered soup pot with the water, a bay leaf and the salt. Bring to a boil then lower heat, partly cover, and simmer about 45 minutes, adding water if necessary, until peas are beginning to fall apart. Remove bay leaf and discard.

Add the chopped onion, celery root, carrots, and potatoes if they are raw (not the mashed ones at this point). Cook partly covered, adding water if necessary, until vegetables are tender. Add the kale, parsley and mashed potatoes if you're adding those.

Continue to simmer another 10 minutes, seasoning with salt and pepper towards the end. If you'd like your *Erwtensoep* to be smooth, process or use a hand blender. Serve with a dab of butter and a little chopped parsley.

SERVES FOUR

Slightly Spanish Kale Soup with Chorizo

2 Tbsp (30 mL) vegetable oil

1 medium onion, chopped

½ lb (225 gr) chorizo sausage in ½-in (1.25-cm) slices

4 large cloves of garlic, minced

2 large 'Yukon Gold' potatoes, peeled and diced

4 cups (1 L) chicken or vegetable stock

2 cups (475 mL) water

1 bay leaf

A few pinches of dried thyme or 1 tsp (5 mL) fresh, minced

1 tsp (5 mL) dried basil

Pinch of dried chili flakes

2 Tbsp (30 mL) tomato paste

4 cups (1 L) kale leaves, loosely packed, chopped

1½ cups (350 mL) cooked chickpeas, drained

Salt and black pepper to taste

Finely chopped cilantro to garnish

*gluten-free if non-gluten sausage is used; vegan if you skip the sausage and use vegetable stock

Look for tomato paste in a tube—it lasts a long time in the fridge and is great if you only need a little. Leave out the chorizo if you want, or substitute turkey sausage or another smoked-type sausage.

In a large stockpot, heat the vegetable oil on medium. Add the onions and sauté about 3 minutes or until onions are slightly translucent. If using it, add chorizo and sauté, stirring, for 5 minutes or until chorizo loses its colour.

Add the garlic and potatoes, continuing to sauté for a few more minutes. Pour in stock and water. Bring to a boil and add bay leaf, thyme, basil, chili flakes and tomato paste. Reduce heat and simmer for about 10 minutes, stirring occasionally.

Add kale and chickpeas, half-cover the pot, and continue to simmer slowly, checking and adding additional water if necessary, for another 20 minutes. Taste for seasoning. Serve garnished with chopped cilantro.

SERVES FOUR TO SIX

White Bean Chowder with Kale & Pumpkin

  *

1 cup (250 mL) dried white beans

1 onion, chopped

2 Tbsp (30 mL) olive oil

1 carrot, chopped

3 garlic cloves

3 Tbsp (45 mL) parsley leaves, finely minced

2 heaping cups (500 mL) pumpkin or winter squash, peeled

6 cups (1.4 L) chicken or vegetable stock, or water

3 cups (700 mL) kale leaves, loosely packed, in chiffonade

2 tsp (10 mL) fresh rosemary, very finely minced

Salt and black pepper

*if vegetable stock is used

If you're like me, you might have small "heels" of grating cheese hanging around in the fridge. This soup begs to have these little bits of Italian-ness added to it during the last part of simmering. Hand-torn crusty, chewy bread rounds out this smooth-tasting potage.

Into a medium pot, put the beans and plenty of water to cover. Bring to a boil, add 2 tsp (10 mL) salt, then simmer for about an hour until al dente but not soft. Set beans aside or refrigerate in their liquid for up to 2 days.

In a heavy-bottomed soup pot with lid, sauté onion in oil for about 5 minutes until translucent. Add the chopped carrots, garlic and parsley and continue to sauté another few minutes until vegetables soften.

Peel the pumpkin or squash, then cut into roughly 1-inch (2.5-cm) cubes. Add to the vegetables, stirring to coat thoroughly. Add the stock or water, bring to a boil, then simmer about 10 minutes until squash is barely tender. Add the kale, drained white beans, rosemary and ground black pepper, extra water if needed, and any heels of cheese you'd like to use. Simmer another 10 minutes.

Remove 2 cups (475 mL) of the soup, and purée using a hand blender or food processor; add back to the soup pot. Let the soup rest for an hour or more before serving. Taste for seasoning, then reheat to serve.

SERVES FOUR TO SIX

Cavolo Nero—Tuscan Black Kale Soup

⅔ lb (about 300 gr) dried cannellini beans

2 tsp (10 mL) salt

5 Tbsp (75 mL) olive oil

2 medium red onions, peeled and finely chopped

2 stalks celery, trimmed and finely chopped

6 cups (1.4 L) Swiss chard in chiffonade

8 cups (2 L) 'Lacinato' (Tuscan) kale in chiffonade

12 cups (3 L) water

Black pepper

1 or 2 small dried chili peppers, crumbled

2 Tbsp (30 mL) tomato paste

Half loaf of day-old Tuscan-style bread, sliced thinly

Very good olive oil for drizzling

*vegan if vegetable stock is used, gluten-free if non-gluten bread is used

Though this is a soup, it's served as a main course in Tuscany. A lovely garden designer named Ayuko Inoue gave me the recipe—she goes to Tuscany every year to help with the olive harvest (sigh. . .). The cavolo nero is a type of 'Lacinato' (aka Tuscan) kale that Italians refer to as "black cabbage." Cannellini beans are bigger and longer than other white beans, so try to find them, as they are traditional.

Don't be put off by what looks like a lot of work. The recipe seems long but each step is easy. If you want to serve the soup Tuscan style in a tureen or bowl, layer the soup and bread at the end until all is used up.

In a large, heavy saucepan, put beans with plenty of water. Bring to a boil, add salt, then lower heat and simmer uncovered for about an hour or until beans are tender, but not falling apart. If the dried beans are older, they'll take longer to reach this stage. Check frequently, stirring occasionally, adding water if necessary.

As beans cook, heat olive oil in stockpot. Add red onion and celery; sweat/sauté until soft but not brown. Add the greens and sauté about 5 to 6 minutes until veggies have softened and reduced in size. Add the 12 cups (3 L) of water, and bring to a slow boil. Add black pepper, crumbled chili pepper and tomato paste. Lower heat and simmer for about 40 minutes.

Toast bread slices in the oven or toaster oven, removing when dry but not brown. Set aside.

Drain the beans, keeping 1 cup (250 mL) of the cooking water. Purée half of the beans with their saved cooking water, leaving the rest of the beans whole. Add both to the stockpot; simmer a further 10 minutes.

To serve, spoon some of the soup into serving dishes, top with a bread slice, then add more soup. Leave to stand a few minutes for the bread to soften, and the flavours to blend before serving. Drizzle with good olive oil, then enjoy.

SERVES EIGHT TO TEN

The "old standby"

Don't overlook plain old kale steamed or cooked in a little water, dressed with butter or olive oil and a squeeze of lemon juice, or sautéed with garlic—the "old standby." Sometimes it's just what the doctor ordered. Meanwhile, here are some other more complex offerings, all starring kale, for your cooking and dining pleasure.

VEGETABLE DISHES & SIDES

Spring Kale Buds with Pancetta & Lemon

 *

3 cups (700 mL) kale buds or more, washed and trimmed

4 Tbsp (60 mL) olive oil, divided

½ cup (125 mL) loosely packed pancetta, diced (optional)

2 Tbsp (30 mL) white wine or water

Juice of 1 lemon

Black pepper to taste

*if you omit the pancetta

Kids love kale buds, and who can blame them? The buds retain their sweetness in spring after having been kissed by frost, so children nibble them like deer at a salad bar. If you don't have kale buds in your garden yet (see our "growing" section), substitute rapini, broccolini or purple sprouting broccoli in this snappy side.

If you can't find pancetta (cured Italian bacon), substitute prosciutto, schinkenspeck or a good Italian salami. Or you can just omit the meat if you wish. Don't be afraid to toss in a few kale flowers.

In a wok or heavy skillet, sauté kale buds in 2 Tbsp (30 mL) oil over medium-high heat, tossing frequently, for about 2 minutes. Remove kale from pan. Add the rest of the oil and cook the pancetta dice until almost crispy.

Return the kale to the pan, add wine or water, and stir-fry 1 to 2 minutes more to combine flavours—kale buds should be al dente.

If you prefer your veggies softer, cover the pot and steam another minute or so. Sprinkle with lemon juice, season with pepper if you like, and serve warm.

SERVES FOUR

Kale Colcannon

4 or 5 large floury potatoes, such as russets, peeled (about 2 lb or 1 kg)

4 cups (1 L) kale leaves, preferably curly, in chiffonade

4 Tbsp (60 mL) butter, divided

½ cup (125 mL) milk

½ cup (125 mL) cream

8 green onions, chopped, including the green parts

1 tsp (5 mL) salt

Black pepper to taste

2 Tbsp (30 mL) parsley, chopped finely

My Irish roots insist that the traditional way of serving kale in Ireland be included. This—rather than desserts made with chocolate or sugar—is my idea of sex in a pan.

Boil the potatoes until tender, drain and set aside. In the same pot, cook the kale in a little water and half the butter until kale is tender—about 8 minutes.

Meanwhile, bring the milk and cream to a boil in a small saucepan. Lower the heat and add the green onions, salt and pepper.

Mash the potatoes, add the hot milk/cream mixture and the kale. Beat well until light and fluffy. Turn out into a warmed bowl, make a well in the centre, and add the rest of the butter, plus a little more, and the chopped parsley.

SERVES FOUR GENEROUSLY

Scalloped Kale with Browned Butter & Sage

2 Tbsp (30 mL) butter

2 large onions, halved, sliced thinly

3–4 cloves garlic, chopped

2 bay leaves

16 cups (4 L) kale, chopped

1 tsp (5 mL) salt

Béchamel Sauce (recipe follows)

Brown Butter:

⅓ cup (80 mL) butter

10–12 fresh sage leaves, washed and chopped finely

*if you make the béchamel sauce with cornstarch or another non-gluten thickener

You can make this cheesy—or not. Either way, it's a lovely rich dish to serve for a special dinner. Leftovers keep well, but there won't be many because it's hard not to have "just another spoonful."

In a heavy skillet, melt butter over medium heat. Sauté onions slowly, stirring frequently, for 10 minutes. Add garlic and bay leaves; continue cooking until onions are soft and fragrant, about 8 more minutes. Do not allow them to brown.

Preheat oven to 400F (205C).

In a large stockpot, steam or cook kale over high heat in salted water for about 5 minutes. Drain, set aside.

Layer sautéed onions into an oiled ovenproof dish, and top with the kale, distributing evenly. Spoon béchamel sauce over and bake about 20 minutes or until sauce is bubbling and the béchamel begins to colour. Remove from oven and let rest while you prepare the browned butter and sage.

TO MAKE BROWN BUTTER:

In a small frying pan (I like to use a cast-iron pan for this), melt the butter and cook over medium-low heat for a few minutes. Add chopped sage and continue to sauté until butter begins to brown.

Drizzle evenly atop scalloped kale.

SERVES SIX TO EIGHT

Béchamel Sauce

 *

3 Tbsp (45 mL) butter

3 Tbsp (45 mL) flour, or cornstarch
or other gluten-free thickener

½ tsp (2.5 mL) salt

2 cups (475 mL) whole milk, heated

A few pinches freshly
grated nutmeg

½ to 1 cup (125–250 mL) assorted
cheese, grated (optional)

*if made with cornstarch or
another non-gluten thickener

If you want to add cheese, go ahead and use up what's in your fridge—Parmigiano-Reggiano, Jarlsberg, cheddar, feta or brie.

Make a roux: in a small saucepan, melt butter, then add thickener and salt. Cook, stirring with a wooden spoon until the roux begins to colour slightly.

Add hot milk a little at a time, beating with a wire whisk thoroughly between additions. Once all the milk is added, switch back to the wooden spoon and cook, stirring, until sauce thickens. Add a few gratings of nutmeg, then stir in cheese if desired.

MAKES ABOUT 2½ CUPS (600 ML)

Tuscan-style Kale-stuffed Giant Shrooms

6 large portobello mushrooms, cleaned

2 Tbsp (30 mL) olive oil plus extra for brushing

parchment paper

¼ cup (60 mL) minced shallots

4 cups (1L) Tuscan kale in chiffonade

¼ cup (60 mL) white wine

Salt and black pepper to taste

3 Tbsp (45 mL) currants or coarsely chopped raisins

¼ cup (60 mL) pine nuts

½ cup (125 mL) grated Pecorino Romano cheese plus extra shavings for garnish

Yolk from a large egg

2 Tbsp (30 mL) panko or fresh fine breadcrumbs or crushed rice crackers

*if you use crushed rice crackers for the crumbs

This is a fitting first course for a more formal occasion or Italianate evening. Should you make this dish in summer and happen to have your own grapevines, line a platter with grape leaves and arrange the portobellos on top. Pinot Noir stands up to the earthy, intense flavours. Offer dense, crusty bread to sop up the juices.

Carefully remove stems from mushrooms. Chop stems coarsely and set aside.

Preheat oven to 400F (205C).

Brush mushroom caps lightly with olive oil and arrange in a single layer in a parchment-lined ovenproof dish. Bake mushrooms 10 to 12 minutes until they begin to soften slightly.

While mushrooms are baking, cook shallots in olive oil in a medium-sized sauté pan, 3 to 4 minutes until softened. Add kale and reserved mushroom stems and sauté about 5 minutes. Add wine, salt and pepper, and cover pan. Cook 5 minutes until kale is tender. Remove from heat; add currants or raisins, pine nuts and grated Pecorino, stirring to combine.

When kale mixture has cooled slightly, beat egg yolk. Add beaten yolk and panko or breadcrumbs to the sauté pan; mix gently. Spoon filling into mushrooms. Bake 15 minutes or until filling is bubbly and lightly browned. Top each portobello with Pecorino shavings.

SERVES SIX

Kale with Apples, Leeks & Feta

1 cup (250 mL) leeks, sliced, including some green

3 Tbsp (45 mL) olive oil, divided

About 4 cups (1L) kale, ribbon-cut into strips

1 large tart apple, cored but unpeeled and quartered lengthwise, sliced into thin wedges

¾ cup (180 mL) crumbled feta cheese

Black pepper

Here's another recipe from Barb Coward, city food-grower extraordinaire. Apple gives the dish sweetness, feta lends depth and acidity and leeks mellow it out. I like to serve this with pork—tenderloin, chops or roast. Tuscan kale gives this stir-fry the most vivid colour.

Stir-fry leeks over medium heat in 2 Tbsp (30 mL) olive oil until they soften—about 2 minutes. Add kale and continue to stir-fry about 4 more minutes.

Turn up the heat to medium-high. Toss in apple slices and continue to cook, stirring frequently for about 3 minutes until apples are tender but not limp. Add feta, grind in a little pepper and toss lightly. Serve drizzled with remaining oil.

SERVES FOUR

A Big Mess o' Winter Greens

*

2 Tbsp (30 mL) olive oil

2 Tbsp (30 mL) butter (or substitute this with more olive oil to make this dish dairy-free)

2 medium onions, chopped

16 cups (4 L) loosely packed kale (can be combined with turnip greens, collards, chard, mustard greens), washed and chopped

Stock, wine or water

1 Tbsp (15 mL) balsamic vinegar, or more to taste

Salt and black pepper

*if olive oil is used instead of butter

Whip up lots of nourishing greens to give your immune system a boost. Roast chicken with rosemary and garlicky mashed potatoes are natural accompaniments.

In a large non-stick sauté pan, melt the butter with the oil. Sauté onions for about 5 minutes over low heat.

Turn the heat to medium-high, add the greens, and cook, stirring until veggies are tender but have not lost their colour—about 8 minutes. If greens dry out, add a little stock, white wine or water.

Stir in the balsamic vinegar and season with salt and pepper.

SERVES EIGHT

Terribly Tuscan Kale with Crispy Salami

1 Tbsp (15 mL) honey or maple syrup

2 tsp (10 mL) balsamic vinegar

Pinch cayenne

3 tsp (15 mL) sea salt

5 cups (1.2 L) Tuscan kale leaves, torn into bite-sized pieces

2 Tbsp (30 mL) olive oil

3 large shallots, peeled, sliced into thin rings

8 thin slices Italian wine salami, cut in narrow strips

Black pepper

This is a unique potluck dish, and a painless way to introduce your carnivore friends to kale. Vary by using prosciutto or lean smoky bacon.

In a small bowl, whisk together honey, vinegar and cayenne. Set aside.

Add about 3 inches (8 cm) of water to a large pot, add salt and bring to a boil. Toss in kale and cook about 3 minutes. Drain, spreading kale on a clean dishtowel to dry.

In a large skillet, heat olive oil over medium heat. Add shallots and stir-fry until they start to colour—about 5 minutes. Remove to a small dish. Increase heat in skillet, add the salami strips and cook until slightly crisp. Transfer the salami to another small dish.

Add kale to skillet and toss quickly—kale should be barely reheated or it will get soggy. Remove from heat, add honey mixture and shallots and toss. Season to taste with pepper. Transfer kale to a warmed serving platter and garnish with the salami.

SERVES FOUR

Wilted Tuscans with Candied Parsnips & Beets

4 cups (about 1 L) Tuscan kale leaves

1 tsp (5 mL) sea salt

1 Tbsp (15 mL) olive oil

4 or 5 small parsnips

2 Tbsp (30 mL) butter plus 1 tsp (5 mL), divided

1 large beet, scrubbed and diced

Stilton, Gorgonzola or blue cheese (optional) as garnish

This simple preparation was inspired by my mother and grand-mother—both loved parsnips prepared this way. Parsnips have an earthy sweetness, especially after a freeze or two, and slow sautéing makes them even more succulent. Staunch parsnip-haters have been converted after eating them—including, most recently, my friend Heather. Not only did she eat all the caramelized parsnips, she then demanded that I caramelize the rest of my raw parsnips from the fridge so she could have more.

The parsnips, beet and kale are distinctly different and complementary in flavour—photogenic and packed with phytonutrients. If you'd rather, serve the beets steamed rather than puréed. Pair with brown rice and grilled fish for a super-healthy dinner.

Massage kale lightly with the salt, then allow kale to rest a few minutes. In a large heavy-bottomed skillet, heat olive oil over medium-high heat, immediately adding kale. Toss and cook gently about a minute until just slightly wilted. Remove kale to colander, and wipe out skillet.

Peel parsnips and cut lengthwise into long, thin pieces. Add 2 Tbsp (30 mL) butter to the skillet and turn heat to medium-high. Cook parsnips, tossing frequently until they begin to caramelize, about 6 minutes.

Meanwhile, cook diced beets in a little water until tender. Drain and reserve some of the highly coloured cooking water. Add to small bowl of food processor (or blender) with about ¼ cup (60 mL) or so of the cooking water and 1 tsp (5 mL) butter. If you want to use a squeeze bottle, fill it with the beet purée. Depending on your squeeze bottle you might need to add a bit more cooking water.

To assemble, decorate individual plates with beet purée, then arrange kale leaves around the plate and top with caramelized parsnips. Add a few bits of cheese if desired.

SERVES FOUR

Squash Mash with Kale & Creamy Onions

  *

4–8 Tbsp (60–120 mL) butter or oil

2 medium onions, sliced thinly

1 lb (454 gr) butternut or other firm orange squash

8 cups (2 L) kale leaves—Gail uses 'Red Russian' but any kind is okay

4 large potatoes, preferably 'Yukon Gold'

Black pepper

*if olive oil is used instead of butter

This is an invention of my friend and neighbour Gail Davidson—tireless human-rights lawyer and enthusiastic gardener. Gail's idea of having someone over for dinner is to invite them, then see what's growing in the garden that day. There's also likely to be a crisp or crumble in the oven made from Gail's own apples, rhubarb or raspberries. Dinners feature kale prominently, as her backyard boasts a veritable 'Red Russian' kale forest.

This is the ultimate comfort food, perfect for a cold winter night. Since the squash is baked just before assembling this dish, it's a good idea to make this when you have something else in the oven—apple or rhubarb crumble, perhaps?

In a large, heavy frying pan melt 2 to 4 Tbsp (30–60 mL) butter on medium heat; add onions, stir-fry a few minutes, then lower the heat. Cook onions very slowly, stirring frequently, for about 20 minutes. Do not allow onions to brown.

Preheat oven to 375F (190C). Cut up squash, wrap in foil, and bake in an ovenproof dish until tender. Keep warm.

Chop kale into 1-inch (2.5-cm) slices and set aside. Peel potatoes, cut in chunks, and boil in lightly salted water until tender. Drain well.

Scrape cooked squash into the cooked potatoes. While potatoes and squash are still warm, add remaining butter and mash until smooth and creamy.

Back to the onions: add a little pepper, then the kale. Turn the heat to medium, put on a lid and steam until the kale is cooked and the water has evaporated.

Spread the potato/squash mixture on a platter or into a ceramic quiche dish and smooth the kale and onions over the top. Serve immediately.

SERVES EIGHT

Provençal Kale & Brussels Sprouts Tian

4 Tbsp (60 mL) olive oil, divided

1 large onion, finely chopped

2 large garlic cloves, minced

1 tsp (5 mL) Herbes de Provence (see following recipe) or fresh thyme leaves

About 8 cups (2 L) kale in chiffonade

1 lb (454 gr) Brussels sprouts, trimmed, sliced thinly into rounds

1 cup (250 mL) soft goat's cheese, crumbled

Black pepper

½ cup (125 mL) milk

½ cup (125 mL) heavy cream

½ cup (125 mL) Gruyère, grated

¼ cup (60 mL) almonds, chopped

½ cup (125 mL) panko or good-quality breadcrumbs

*if non-gluten bread is used for the crumbs

"Tian" refers to both the baking dish and the layered arrangement of vegetables with a savoury crunch of crumbs adorning the top. Herbes de Provence lends authenticity to the dish—I've included a recipe easily made in summer using herbs from your own kitchen garden.

Preheat oven to 375F (190C).

Oil a two-quart gratin dish. Heat 2 Tbsp (30 mL) olive oil in a large, heavy non-stick skillet over medium heat. Add onions and sauté slowly, cooking until onions are translucent and sweet, about 10 minutes. Add garlic and herbs and sauté another minute or two.

Add the kale still wet from washing and ½ tsp (2.5 mL) salt. Cook and stir until kale begins to wilt, about 4 minutes. Add about ¼ cup (60 mL) of water and cook another few minutes, stirring. Remove kale/onion mixture to a bowl and set aside.

Cook Brussels sprouts in the same pan in 2 Tbsp (30 mL) oil over medium-high. Sauté sprouts a few minutes, adding a pinch or two of salt and a little water. Cover and steam for 3 or 4 minutes. Remove sprouts, drain and set aside.

Assemble tian: put half the kale into the baking dish, then half the Brussels sprouts, pressing down to make even layers. Arrange the crumbled goat's cheese evenly on top, grind a little pepper on, then add the next layers of kale and sprouts.

Mix the milk and cream together, then drizzle over the tian. Whirl Gruyère, almonds and breadcrumbs in food processor or chop finely. Strew evenly over top. Bake about 40 minutes or until firm and golden brown. Allow to rest 15 minutes before serving.

SERVES SIX

Herbes de Provence

Use fresh herbs, chopped finely with a sharp knife. In a bowl, mix together approximately:

3 Tbsp (45 mL) each of rosemary, thyme, marjoram, summer savory and basil leaves

About 2 tsp (10 mL) fresh lavender buds

Cut-up bay leaves (optional)

Fennel seed (optional)

Alas—my wonderful friend and tenant, Marion Carpentier, crazy backcountry skier, ballerina and volcanologist, has returned to France. Among the wonderful things M brought was a herb blend from her home in Brittany by the sea.

This approximation will be easy for you to whip up and if you have these herbs in your garden, so much the better. Do make this heady herb mélange in midsummer, when fresh herbs are plentiful. Use in the Provencal Kale and Brussels Sprouts Tian, or rub all over a plump free-range chicken before roasting.

Be sure to make extra for much-appreciated gifts. Quantities can be easily multiplied and are not written in stone.

Dry in a dehydrator if you have one, or on a screen in an airy warm place like your porch, or in a very slow oven—be prepared to be transported by the wafting scent. When herbs are dry, rub them with your hands (my favourite part) to pulverize, or run through a blender briefly. Store the herbs in a jar with tight-fitting lid.

MAKES ABOUT 1 CUP (250 ML)

Kale with Braised Winter Squash, Pears & Bacon

1 large 'Delicata' squash (or other winter squash)

1 Tbsp (15 mL) olive oil

2 slices smoky bacon or pancetta, chopped

1 medium onion, finely chopped

6 fresh sage leaves, coarsely chopped

Salt and black pepper

1 cup (250 mL) pear cider plus extra in case pan dries out

1 Tbsp (15 mL) white wine vinegar

1 tsp (5 mL) sugar

1 ripe but firm pear—'Bartlett', 'Bosc' or red—unpeeled, cored, quartered

6 cups (1.4 L) kale leaves

If you use 'Delicata' squash, there's no need to peel it as the skin is tender and edible. Yummy with roast chicken and garlic mash, this dish cries out for a lovely, slightly flinty BC Pinot Gris.

Cut squash in half. Remove seeds and chop into 1-inch (2.5-cm) dice.

Heat olive oil in a large sauté pan (equipped with lid) over medium heat. Cook bacon to your desired crispness, tossing frequently. Remove bacon, drain and set aside. Add onions to pan and sauté 3 to 4 minutes. Add squash, sage, salt and pepper. Stir and sauté to coat squash well with onions and herbs. Add pear cider, vinegar and sugar. Bring to a boil, then lower heat and simmer, covered, for 5 minutes.

Slice the pear quarters lengthwise into thin slices. Add pear slices and kale to the pan. Cover and simmer for 10 to 15 minutes, stirring occasionally, until squash is tender. If pan appears dry, add a little more cider. Turn into serving dish and top with reserved bacon.

SERVES FOUR

PASTA, POLENTA & RISOTTO

Easiest Kale Pasta

Pasta of your choice

Kale

* gluten-free if non-gluten pasta
is used; vegan without cheese

If you are, shall we say, "acquainting certain family members un-awares" with kale, this is a good place to start. Just put in a little at first, and tell them it's parsley.

While boiling any pasta the way you normally would, add a few handfuls of finely chopped kale for the last 2 to 3 minutes of cooking time. When pasta is to your liking, drain kale and pasta, and serve with a favourite sauce or simply anoint with good olive oil and a little freshly grated Parmigiano-Reggiano, Asiago or Pecorino Romano.

Pasta Puttanesca with Kale

2 Tbsp (30 mL) olive oil

1 small tin anchovies (or less, or none if you prefer)

4 cloves garlic, chopped fine

3 cups (700 mL) kale in chiffonade

⅓ cup (80 mL) white wine

12 Castelvetrano olives, pitted by hand into pieces

Pinch chili flakes or 1 tiny dried chili, finely chopped

Zest of ½ lemon

Juice of 1 lemon

10.5 oz (300 gr) spaghetti or spaghettini

½ cup (125 mL) Parmigiano-Reggiano, grated

Salt and black pepper

*vegetarian if you leave out the anchovies; gluten-free if non-gluten pasta is used

Since the other ingredients are inexpensive, why not use real Parmigiano-Reggiano or Padano? A little goes a long way. Ditto the olives, which are Sicilian in origin. If you can't find Castelvetrano olives, another green kind is fine, or use your favourite. 'Lacinato' kale makes the pasta the brightest green.

In a heavy-bottomed skillet over medium heat, sauté the anchovies in olive oil until dissolved. Turn the heat down to medium-low, then add the garlic and sauté about 30 seconds—don't allow it to brown. Toss in the kale and sauté until kale is wilted but still green, about 3 minutes. Add wine and cook a few more minutes until the alcohol evaporates. Quickly toss olives, chili, lemon zest and juice into the skillet then remove pan from heat.

Bring a large pot of salted water to a boil and add pasta. Cook until al dente or to your taste.

Drain pasta and place in heated serving bowl, add kale mixture, Parmigiano-Reggiano, and salt and pepper to taste. Serve with extra cheese.

SERVES TWO FOR DINNER OR FOUR AS A STARTER

Kale & Goats with Bows

6 large garlic cloves, peeled

2 or 3 small shallots, peeled

8 cups (2 L) kale leaves, packed

12 oz (about 350 gr) dried farfalle
(bowtie pasta)

8 oz (225 gr) soft goat's cheese,
plus extra for topping

3 Tbsp (45 mL) pine nuts

Salt and black pepper

3 Tbsp (45 mL) lemon juice

½ cup (125 mL) extra virgin olive oil

Fresh thyme leaves (optional)

*if non-gluten pasta is used

Not goats, but goat's cheese. Just trying to keep you awake! Any variety of kale is fine in this easy pasta dish—everything is cooked in one pot. Feel free to use mature leaves as they'll be whirled with goat cheese to create a strikingly green pesto that melts into the hot pasta. If you have calendula in your garden, be sure to garnish the pasta with some edible orange petals—nasturtiums work too.

Bring a large pot of salted water to a boil. Add the garlic and shallots and boil gently for 4 minutes. Add kale leaves and continue to boil for another minute. Watch the pot—you want the kale to remain bright green.

Using a slotted spoon, remove kale to a colander. Scoop out the garlic and shallots and transfer them to the bowl of a food processor. Leave pot with water at a boil. Drop pasta into the boiling water.

While pasta is cooking, squeeze excess moisture from kale. Add to food processor along with the cheese, pine nuts, salt, pepper and lemon juice. Process while adding olive oil slowly, until mixture is creamy. Let pesto mixture stand until pasta is cooked to the desired texture.

Drain pasta well and combine with puréed mixture. Before serving, sprinkle with extra goat's cheese and fresh thyme leaves if you have them.

SERVES FOUR AS A MAIN COURSE

Mushroom & Pancetta Linguine with Wilted Kale

12 oz (about 350 gr) dried linguine or pasta of your choice

8 oz (225 gr) mushrooms, washed and chopped

2 Tbsp (30 mL) olive oil or butter

2 or 3 small shallots, peeled

A few sprigs fresh thyme or 1 tsp (5 mL) dried thyme

2 oz (50 gr) (8–10 paper-thin slices) pancetta or prociutto, quartered

4 cups (1 L) young kale leaves, or a mixture of kale and chard in chiffonade

1 Tbsp (15 mL) balsamic vinegar or wine

Salt and black pepper

Grated Parmigiano-Reggiano, Asiago or Romano for garnish

*gluten-free if served with non-gluten pasta; vegetarian without the pancetta; vegan if olive oil is used instead of butter and without the pancetta and cheese

Here's a quick and easy autumn supper. This will work with store-bought mushrooms, but if you can find some wild ones it makes the dish really special. If you prefer your kale softer or the leaves are very mature, you could add it to the pasta during the last three minutes of cooking instead of wilting it in the pan. For a vegetarian meal, substitute something salty for the ham, like a handful of thinly sliced sundried tomatoes or chopped olives.

Bring a large pot of salted water to a boil and cook pasta according to package directions.

While pasta is cooking, place a large skillet over high heat (without oil) until very hot, then add the chopped mushrooms and a good pinch of salt. Cook over high heat, stirring occasionally until most of the water has evaporated and the mushrooms begin to brown and stick to the pan, then add butter or oil and shallots, thyme and pancetta. Immediately reduce heat to medium and, stirring occasionally, cook until shallots are tender. Add the kale, and sauté for 2 minutes until kale wilts, deglazing with a splash of balsamic vinegar or wine. Season with salt and pepper and transfer mixture to a warm serving bowl.

Drain pasta well and combine with kale and mushroom mixture. Before serving, sprinkle with grated cheese and more ground pepper.

SERVES FOUR FOR DINNER

Kale & Ricotta Lasagna

One recipe Béchamel Sauce (page 140)

2 Tbsp (30 mL) olive oil

1 small onion, finely chopped

3 cloves garlic, minced

2 cups (475 mL) thick tomato sauce or crushed tomatoes (not tomato paste)

1 bay leaf

1 tsp (5 mL) fresh rosemary, minced (don't use dry)

½ cup (125 mL) red or white wine

1 cup (250 mL) parsley including thinner stems, finely chopped

1 cup (250 mL) ricotta cheese

1 cup (250 mL) Asiago or Parmigiano (Reggiano or Padano) or other semi-hard Italian cheese, grated

1 egg, lightly beaten

½ tsp (2.5 mL) salt

Black pepper

1 Tbsp butter (15 mL) or olive oil for frying the kale

6 cups (1.4 L) or up to 8 cups (2 L) kale leaves and tender stems, chopped finely

12 Barilla no-cook egg noodles

Extra grated cheese for topping the lasagna (optional)

This is easy (for lasagna) and delicious—those who've tried it wildly agree. It's made with "no cook" noodles, in this case Barilla egg lasagna (*lasagne all'uovo*), which you should be able to find at a large grocery store or Italian deli. They are thin and smaller than the usual lasagna noodles, two of them fitting a 9-inch (about 23-cm) square pan perfectly, and contain only two ingredients: semolina and eggs. No need to make the sauce extra watery, either.

From the different languages on the package it seems these noodles are available worldwide, but if you can't find them, use the noodles you are accustomed to. A little extra nutmeg in the béchamel accentuates the kale.

Prepare Béchamel Sauce; set aside.

Make the tomato sauce: Heat the oil in a skillet over medium-low. Add onions and sauté 5 minutes, stirring. Add garlic and sauté for another 3 minutes. Add crushed tomatoes, 2 cups (475 mL) water, bay leaf and rosemary. Simmer 5 minutes, then add the wine and the parsley and simmer another 10 minutes. Sauce should be "saucey" but not watery; add a little water if necessary. Remove bay leaf; let the sauce rest.

Mix the ricotta and Asiago (or other cheese), the beaten egg and salt and pepper in a medium bowl. Set aside. Heat the oil over medium-high in a large skillet or pot and sauté the kale for 2 minutes until softened. Add 2 Tbsp (30 mL) water, then cover and steam for another minute. Remove kale with a slotted spoon. It's fine for it to be moist.

Preheat oven to 350F (175C). Oil the sides of a deep 9-inch (23-cm) square ovenproof dish.

Continued from previous page.

ASSEMBLE LASAGNA:

Spread a few spoonfuls of béchamel evenly over the bottom of the pan. Cover with two noodles.

Add about one third of the tomato sauce, then cover with two noodles. Lay noodles in the same direction and not crossed.

Add half the ricotta mixture. Top with half the kale, smoothing to even out the layers. Cover with two noodles again.

Add another third of the tomato sauce, and two more noodles.

Add the rest of the ricotta, the rest of the kale, and two more noodles.

Add the rest of the tomato sauce and two final noodles. Cover with the remaining béchamel, smoothing out the top. Sprinkle with more cheese if you like.

Bake about 30 minutes or until bubbly and beginning to brown at the edges. Allow the lasagna to sit for at least 15 minutes before slicing—longer is better. You can then reheat the whole works in the oven. It's also fine to make it earlier in the day (or the day before) if you really want the layers to be distinct.

SERVES SIX GENEROUSLY

Pizzoccheri

3 cups (700 mL) kale leaves, chopped

2 cups (475 mL) cabbage, coarsely chopped

2 potatoes, peeled, quartered and sliced

About ¾ lb (350 gr) pizzoccheri or wide whole-wheat noodles

1 cup (250 mL) Fontina, preferably Val d'Aosta, chopped or coarsely grated

½ cup (125 mL) Parmigiano-Reggiano, grated

1 cup (250 mL) breadcrumbs made from good-quality bread

1 recipe Browned Butter with Sage (page 139)

My friend Karin Ward and I first made pizzoccheri when we found dried pasta noodles made with buckwheat. "Pizzocheri," native to Valtellina in the Lombardy region of Italy, describes both the noodles and the finished dish. That was a while back, and although I have searched high and low, those buckwheat noodles are nowhere to be seen (except for skinny little soba noodles). I'm giving you the recipe anyway, hoping you can find them! They are available fresh, frozen or dried—in New York. (If you don't live in the Big Apple, you wanted to go there, didn't you?)

In the meantime, substitute broad whole-wheat or farro pasta, or lasagna noodles broken into uneven pieces. Or you can even make these easy buckwheat noodles yourself, with instructions straight from the Accademia del Pizzocchero. Simply mix four parts buckwheat with one part white flour. Add a little water, and knead for a few minutes. Roll thin with a rolling pin and cut with a knife into noodles.

This super-easy, super-delicious peasant fare is cooked in one pot, baked briefly, and slathered with browned butter and crispy sage leaves. Mamma mia!

Bring a large pot of salted water to a boil. Add the kale, cabbage and potatoes. Keep at a steady low boil for about 6 minutes. Add the noodles and continue to cook another 10 minutes until noodles are tender. Drain (save the cooking water for soup) and set aside.

Preheat the oven to 350F (175C). Grease a 2 to 3 quart (2 to 3 L) ovenproof dish. Layer a third of the kale/noodle mixture on the bottom, and sprinkle half the Fontina and Parmigiano-Reggiano evenly over the first layer. Add another third of the kale mixture, then the rest of the cheese. Spoon the last third of the kale mixture on top, then strew breadcrumbs evenly over the top of your pizzoccheri. Drizzle with Browned Butter. Bake about 20 minutes or until top is browned and your pizzoccheri is bubbling and fragrant. Enjoy with a glass or two of Italian red.

SERVES FOUR

Creamy Polenta with Kale & Slow-roasted Tomatoes

2 lb (900 gr) 1½- to 2-inch (3- to 5-cm) tomatoes like 'Campari' or another smallish type, halved

Sea salt

Black pepper

Small sprigs of seasonal fresh herbs—rosemary, thyme, basil, tarragon

2 or 3 cloves garlic, cut into slivers

Olive oil

6 slices (1-inch or 2.5-cm thick) of butternut or other firm, brightly-coloured squash

2 tsp (10 mL) salt

1¾ cup (about 400 mL) cornmeal (I prefer the paler stoneground organic cornmeal for the polenta rather than the bright yellow stuff)

3 Tbsp (45 mL) unsalted butter

½ cup (125 mL) Asiago, Romano or other hard Italian grating cheese plus extra for serving

18 spears asparagus, fibrous stems removed by snapping

18–24 Tuscan kale leaves, stems removed

Slow-roasting tomatoes brings out their depth and sweetness, and if you could bottle the smell and sell it, you might make a million. Since the oven is on for hours, I suggest you prepare more tomatoes than you need for the polenta; use extra for sandwiches, bruschetta, pizza (like the Kale Lavash on page 95) or pasta. The tomatoes disappear mysteriously from the kitchen as well. If you can't find 'Campari', substitute small 'Roma' types or large 'Grape' varieties. This combination of veggies offers a powerhouse of phytonutrients and vitamins, in a most palatable and beautiful way.

Preheat oven to 200F (100C).

Arrange tomatoes, cut side up, on a large parchment-covered cookie sheet. Sprinkle lightly with salt and pepper. Tuck small herb leaves and a tiny sliver or two of garlic into each tomato half, and drizzle lightly with olive oil.

Oil the squash pieces. Wrap in foil and place on cookie sheet with tomatoes. Place cookie sheet in centre of the oven and cook for 1 hour.

Check to ensure the tomatoes aren't drying up too quickly, then continue roasting them for up to one and a half more hours. The squash should be tender by this time as well. (Tomatoes can be made a day or two ahead—allow them to cool, then refrigerate.)

Continued from previous page.

To prepare the polenta, bring 6 cups (1.4 L) water to a boil in a large, heavy saucepan. Add salt, then gradually whisk in cornmeal. Reduce heat to low and cook, stirring regularly, until mixture thickens and cornmeal is tender—about 15 minutes. Remove from heat and stir in butter and cheese, combining well.

As you cook the polenta, steam the asparagus and the kale in very little water in a covered frying pan until both veggies are tender but still brightly coloured. Drain, and assemble plate: spoon polenta onto pre-warmed platter, flattening it a little, then drape kale leaves around polenta, and arrange roasted tomatoes, squash and asparagus spears artfully on the platter. Top with more cheese if desired.

SERVES SIX

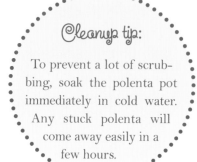

Cleanup tip:

To prevent a lot of scrubbing, soak the polenta pot immediately in cold water. Any stuck polenta will come away easily in a few hours.

Relaxed Risotto with Kale, Garlic & Wild Mushrooms

 *

½ oz (15 gr) dried mushrooms or 7 oz (200 gr) fresh

5 cups (1.2 L) vegetable or chicken stock

5 or 6 large cloves garlic, peeled (not chopped)

1 Tbsp (15 mL) olive oil

1 Tbsp (15 mL) butter

1 cup (250 mL) onion, diced

1 cup (250 mL) plus 2 Tbsp (30 mL) Arborio rice

½ cup (125 mL) white wine

4 cups (1 L) kale leaves tightly packed, in chiffonade

½ cup (125 mL) Parmigiano-reggiano, grated, plus extra for serving

Salt (optional—store-bought stock is usually salty enough)

Black pepper

*if vegetable stock is used

With apologies to Marcella Hazan, you don't have to slave over a hot stove to produce good risotto. Stir occasionally—even put the lid on for a minute or two or add two ladlefuls of broth at once. Porcini, chanterelles, shiitake—a small amount of wild mushrooms makes this risotto rich and flavourful.

If using dried mushrooms, reconstitute as directed. Drain, saving the liquid for the risotto, and chop the mushrooms finely. If using fresh, clean the mushrooms carefully, slice and set aside.

Bring stock to a simmer in a saucepan. Add peeled garlic cloves to stock and cook about 5 minutes. Remove garlic, chop or mash and set aside.

In a heavy-bottomed saucepan over medium-low heat, sauté the onions in oil and butter until softened but not browned, stirring frequently for about 5 minutes. Increase heat to medium; add the rice and sauté until well coated. Begin to ladle hot stock into the rice a little at a time, stirring well with a wooden spoon, scraping the bottom of the pan regularly. The rice will take up liquid and begin to soften. Add the reserved mushroom liquid if this applies, then keep stirring and adding stock. If you like, you can put the lid on, turn the heat down quite low, and walk away from the stove occasionally.

When you've added about half the stock, add the mushrooms, their liquid, the wine, the reserved garlic and the kale. Continue stirring, adding stock until the risotto is to your liking—al dente, or creamy. Add the cheese and black pepper and salt (if needed) to taste. Stir well, and serve the risotto immediately with extra cheese.

SERVES TWO AS A MAIN COURSE, FOUR AS A SIDE

MAINS

Kale, Salmon & Potato Cakes

4 cups (1 L) mashed potatoes

¼ tsp (1 mL) black pepper

½ tsp (2.5 mL) salt

1 tsp (5 mL) dried dillweed, or more if it's fresh

¼ tsp (1 mL) grated nutmeg

2 cups (475 mL) kale, very finely chopped

¼ cup (60 mL) parsley, finely chopped

2 eggs, lightly beaten

¼ cup (60 mL) green onions, minced

⅔ cup (160 mL) grated cheese, preferably Swiss, Asiago or Piave

One 1-lb (418 gr) can wild salmon, drained and flaked

Oil for frying—preferably grapeseed, olive or another good vegetable oil

Panko or gluten-free cracker crumbs

*if gluten-free cracker crumbs are used

This is a yummy and nutritious way to make good use of leftover mashed potatoes, ditto if you have extra cooked salmon left from oven roasting or the barbecue. Eat them for lunch, or form smaller patties and serve them as appetizers or snacks. You can vary the recipe by adding corn and serving with salsa and sour cream—omit the nutmeg and add a pinch of cumin and chili powder—olé!

If you can't find the large cans of salmon, use two regular-sized ones.

Scrub up and use your hands to mix everything except the oil and panko together in a large-ish bowl. Form the mixture into flattened cakes 2 inches (5 cm) wide, then roll in panko or gluten-free cracker crumbs. Fry the patties about 3 minutes per side in an oiled cast-iron or other heavy skillet until nicely browned on both sides.

MAKES ABOUT FOURTEEN CAKES

Moussaka with Kale & Lamb

1 large, firm eggplant—about
1 lb (454 gr)

Salt

Vegetable oil for frying

1 small onion, finely chopped

1 Tbsp (15 mL) vegetable oil

1 lb (454 gr) lean ground lamb

½ tsp (2.5 mL) dried oregano

½ tsp (2.5 mL) ground cinnamon

1 bay leaf

½ cup (125 mL) chicken
stock or water

¼ cup (60 mL) white wine

3 medium 'Yukon Gold' potatoes—
about 1 lb (454 gr)

8 cups (2 L) tightly packed kale
leaves in chiffonade

1 recipe Béchamel Sauce (page 140)

2 egg yolks

*if you make the Béchamel
Sauce with cornstarch or another
non-gluten thickener

This is a rich dish, and you do have to fry eggplant—but it's so worth it. If you love béchamel sauce, double the recipe and use extra on top of the moussaka. You can always make any leftovers into a cheese sauce. If you must, substitute ground turkey for the lamb, though I daresay it won't taste quite as "Greek." This dish keeps well in the fridge for up to three days.

Environmentalists will want to have recycled paper towels or brown paper grocery bags on hand as this recipe does use a few of them to soak up excess oil from the eggplant.

Slice eggplant crosswise in ½-inch (1.25-cm) slices. Salt both sides lightly and place in a colander to drain for half an hour or so. Rinse and pat the eggplant dry with paper towels. In a non-stick skillet, using a little oil, fry the eggplant rounds a few at a time, turning once, until lightly browned on each side. As eggplants are cooked, place them on another paper towel.

Using the same skillet, sauté the onion in oil over medium heat for a few minutes, then add the ground lamb, oregano, cinnamon and bay leaf. Using a fork, break up the lamb as it cooks until the meat begins to lose its colour. Add the chicken stock and wine, simmering for 5 minutes or until the alcohol evaporates. Remove the bay leaf. Transfer the lamb to a rectangular ovenproof dish with sides more than 3 inches (7.5 cm) high. Place the eggplant slices evenly over the lamb, forming a second layer.

Over

Continued from previous page.

Peel and quarter the potatoes, slice them the width of your baby finger and cook in a pot of salted water until tender but not falling apart. Remove with a slotted spoon and put a layer of potatoes atop the eggplant as evenly as possible.

Add the kale to the potato pot and cook about 5 minutes until tender. Drain well, squeezing out the liquid—and, although I might have said it once or twice before, be sure to save the potato and kale cooking water for soup. Place the kale evenly over the potato layer.

Preheat oven to 350F (175C).

Prepare the Béchamel Sauce (page 140). When it has cooled slightly, beat in 2 egg yolks. Spoon over the moussaka. Bake about 25 minutes, or until the moussaka is bubbling at the edges and nicely browned. Remove from oven and allow it to cool and firm up for 10 minutes before serving.

SERVES FOUR TO SIX

Coco-nutty Fish 'n' Kale

2 Tbsp (30 mL) coconut oil

1 shallot, minced

2 cloves garlic, minced

2 Tbsp (30 mL) ginger root, minced

3 cups (700 mL) kale leaves in chiffonade

2 cups (475 mL) very fresh bean sprouts, well rinsed

1¾ cup (400 mL) coconut milk

½ cup (125 mL) water or stock

12 oz (about 350 gr) sole filets

As mentioned before, every so often a recipe happens because of what's in the fridge, and that's how this concoction came about. I served my Coco-nutty Fish 'n' Kale with "Forbidden Rice"—black and unhulled and evidently super high in antioxidants. It harmonizes particularly well with all the coconut flavours. If you can't find this rice, wehani or jasmine rice would be just fine too.

In a skillet fitted with a cover, melt the coconut oil over medium heat. Sauté the shallot, garlic and ginger root, stirring, about 5 minutes. Add the kale and sauté another 5 minutes or until it's slightly tender but still bright green.

Add the bean sprouts, distributing them evenly over the top of the kale, then pour the coconut milk and water or stock over all. Place the fish pieces on top of the bean sprouts. Cover the pan and steam over low heat for about 8 minutes or until fish is cooked to your liking. Serve with cooked rice.

SERVES TWO

Turkey Burgers with Microgreens

1 lb (454 gr) ground turkey

½ tsp (5 mL) salt

Black pepper to taste

½ cup (125 mL) cilantro, finely chopped

¼ cup (60 mL) parsley, minced

¼ cup (60 mL) mint, finely chopped

½ cup (125 mL) finely chopped kale leaves

1 egg, beaten with 2 tsp (10 mL) water

½ cup (125 mL) panko or other fresh breadcrumbs

Kale microgreens for garnish

Oil for frying

4 buns and "the fixings"

*if you use non-gluten crumbs and buns

If you're pressed for time, chop the greens (the ones in the burgers, not the microgreens) in your food processor, add the egg, salt and black pepper, give it a blast, then add the turkey and breadcrumbs and process briefly. Voilà! Try these with the Gorgeous Green Chutney on page 94. Read up on how to grow kale microgreens on page 47.

In a medium bowl, mix all ingredients except microgreens, oil, and buns with your hands to incorporate well; do not overmix, lest your burgers become tough.

Shape into four patties; fry in oil about 4–5 minutes on each side, depending on thickness. If it's barbecue season, brush the burgers with a little oil before grilling as they don't have much (if any) fat.

Garnish with microgreens and "the fixings"—whatever those are for you.

MAKES FOUR TURKEY BURGERS

Black-eyed Peas & Kale with Smoky Bacon

1 lb (454 gr) dried black-eyed peas

6 cups (1.4 L) water

1 tsp (5 mL) salt

1 good-sized jalapeño pepper (deveined, seeded, chopped)

4 oz (125 gr) pancetta or smoky bacon in 1-inch (2.5-cm) dice

1 Tbsp (15 mL) vegetable oil

1 large onion, diced

3 cloves garlic, chopped

8 cups (2 L) kale leaves, packed

2 cups (475 mL) collards and/or chard, packed

Hot sauce (optional)

This makes a southern-style meal with complete protein if you serve it with cornbread or polenta (see recipe page 163). Wear rubber gloves or at least be cautious when cutting the jalapeño—and be careful not to touch your eyes or mouth as I did when I made it.

Wash black-eyed peas; place in a large pot with the water, salt and jalapeño. Bring to a boil, then lower heat to simmer, cover and cook for 45 minutes or until peas are tender. Check occasionally to make sure there's enough liquid. Keep the black-eyed peas warm.

While peas cook, sauté the pancetta or bacon in oil in a large saucepan with lid over medium heat until lightly browned, about 5 minutes. Add onions and garlic, sautéing another 5 minutes, stirring often.

Chop kale and collards in bite-sized pieces. Chop the tender parts of stems as well, in ½-inch (1.25-cm) lengths. Wash the greens, leaving them quite wet, and add them to the bacon, onions and garlic. Depending on the size of your pot, you may have to push the greens down but they'll quickly wilt. Cover and cook, stirring occasionally until greens are softened—about 10 minutes.

To serve, add the kale mixture to the beans. Stir and cook together about 5 minutes, and add hot sauce if desired.

SERVES FOUR GENEROUSLY

Thai Chicken Curry

2 tsp (10 mL) coconut oil

3 garlic cloves, minced

1 Tbsp (15 mL) fresh ginger root, minced

2 Tbsp (30 mL) red curry paste (or to taste)

3 dried Kaffir lime leaves (optional)

1¾ cup (400 mL) coconut milk

2 tsp (10 mL) brown sugar

2 cups (475 mL) chicken stock

2 chicken breasts cut in bite-sized chunks

6 cups (1.4 L) kale leaves in chiffonade

½ lb (225 gr) fresh or frozen green beans

1 can bamboo shoots

1 sweet red bell pepper, deveined and sliced thinly

Cooked jasmine rice or rice noodles

Fresh cilantro leaves, chopped, for garnish

1 lime, in wedges

Whenever I cook with curry paste, I think of my oldest son, Jesse. Cooking Thai curry one evening in his home in Calgary, I managed to fill the place with a burning odour and we had to run outside in order to breathe. Phew! Thank you to Stacey Deering and her Paleo-Diet website for adding kale to Thai curry; if you'd rather use chicken thighs or part of a whole chicken, go right ahead.

In a heavy-bottomed skillet, melt the coconut oil over medium heat. Add the garlic, ginger, curry paste and lime leaves to the pan, and sauté about 5 minutes. At this point, breathe through your mouth instead of your nose just in case, and/or open the window. Add the coconut milk a little at a time to the pan, stirring. Add the brown sugar and chicken stock and cook, stirring, until mixture thickens slightly—about 5 minutes.

Add the chicken and kale, simmering another 5 minutes. Toss in the green beans and bamboo shoots, and simmer yet another 5 minutes. Then add the sliced bell peppers and cook just 1–2 minutes, ensuring the peppers stay slightly crisp. Serve atop cooked rice and garnish with cilantro. Pass lime sections so diners can add a squeeze at the last minute, and enjoy.

SERVES FOUR

Corny Kale Enchiladas con Pollo

Enchilada sauce (see recipe on p. 178)

2 Tbsp (30 mL) vegetable oil

½ cup (125 mL) finely chopped yellow onion

2 cloves garlic, chopped

1 tsp (5 mL) ground cumin

1 cup (250 mL) corn kernels (frozen or fresh)

3 cups (700 mL) kale leaves in chiffonade

⅓ cup (80 mL) green chile sauce (canned or bottled)

3 Tbsp (45 mL) masa harina or corn flour

1 cup (250 mL) goat's or other soft white cheese in bits

1 cup (250 mL) cooked chicken, chopped

12 large corn tortillas, preferably organic

Oil for frying

Grated white or orange cheese for topping

Fresh cilantro, chopped, for garnish

I love enchiladas, and although these ones are healthier than some, due to the kale and corn, they're still pretty decadent-tasting. Purchase a decent enchilada sauce if you are not in the mood to make your own. Serve the enchiladas with rice and a salad—with kale, of course.

Have a pan with Enchilada Sauce simmering at the ready.

Prepare filling: in a medium-large skillet, sauté onion, garlic and cumin in the oil. Add the corn, stir-fry 3-4 minutes. Add kale and continue to cook and stir for 5 minutes. If the pan becomes dry, add a little water. Add green chile sauce, masa harina, cheese and chicken. Combine, and set aside.

Preheat oven to 375F (190C). Fry tortillas in medium-hot oil briefly until softened, about 20 seconds on each side. Dip into warm enchilada sauce, and lay on a cutting board or large plate. Place a good-sized spoonful of filling along the bottom edge of the tortilla, and roll. Place seam-side down, side by side, in a greased ovenproof casserole. If there is filling left over, tuck it in around the sides of the rolled tortillas or roll a few more.

Pour on the rest of the sauce. Bake 10 minutes, remove from oven and sprinkle the top with cheese. Bake another 10 minutes until filling is bubbly and cheese is melted. Let stand about 10 minutes before dishing out; garnish with chopped fresh cilantro and serve with sour cream and more green sauce if desired.

SERVES SIX

Enchilada Sauce

1 Tbsp (15 mL) vegetable oil

½ cup (125 mL) onions, finely chopped

2–3 cloves garlic, chopped

1 tsp (5 mL) dried oregano

1 tsp (5 mL) cumin powder

½ tsp (2.5 mL) cinnamon

3 Tbsp (45 mL) masa harina, corn flour or fine cornmeal

¼ cup (60 mL) chili powder (hot or mild—whatever you prefer)

3½ cups (825 mL) vegetable stock or water

1 Tbsp (15 mL) good-quality cocoa powder

Use for any kind of enchilada—it's easy to make and way better than canned.

In a saucepan or skillet over medium-high, sauté onion in oil until translucent. Add garlic, oregano, cumin and cinnamon, then stir-fry 3 more minutes. Add masa harina (or cornmeal) and chili powder. Cook and stir until sauce begins to thicken. Whisk in stock or water. Simmer 5 minutes, add cocoa, and simmer another few minutes.

MAKES ABOUT 4 CUPS (1 L)

Kale Shepherd's Pie with Lentils

2 Tbsp (30 mL) vegetable oil

2 cups (475 mL) carrots, diced

1 large red onion or 2 small, chopped

4 cloves garlic, minced

1 tsp (5 mL) fresh rosemary, minced, or a pinch of dried (not too much!)

3 fresh sage leaves, finely minced

½ cup (125 mL) parsley, minced

1½ cups (350 mL) green lentils, washed

Black pepper

4 cups (1 L) water

1 cup (250 mL) canned tomatoes, chopped

1 tsp (5 mL) salt

1½ lb (about 700 gr) potatoes, preferably 'Yukon Gold'

1 lb (454 gr) yams (or sweet potatoes)

½ cup (125 mL) milk

3 Tbsp (45 mL) butter

1¼ cups (about 300 mL) cheddar cheese, grated, divided

8 cups (2 L) kale leaves in chiffonade

This is a perfect potluck offering as the nutritious ingredients will keep everyone going for days. If you'd like, add an egg yolk or two to the mashed layer and feel free to play with other root veggies for the topping too. Celeriac, parsnips or turnips would be equally yummy.

In a large skillet with lid sauté the carrots, red onions, garlic, rosemary, sage and parsley in the oil until vegetables soften. Add the lentils and pepper, stirring to mix well. Add water, tomatoes and salt, bring mixture to a boil, then lower heat and simmer, covered, for about 30 minutes or until lentils are tender, adding water if needed.

While lentil mixture cooks, cut the potatoes and yams into 2-inch (5-cm) chunks. Cook in salted water until tender, about 15 minutes. Drain (save the liquid) and mash with the milk, butter and half the cheese, then set aside.

Transfer lentil mixture to a large oiled ovenproof dish. Using the same skillet, steam the kale with a little water and a pinch of salt, covered, for 5 minutes or until tender. Drain well and layer evenly on top of lentil mixture. Preheat oven to 350F (175C).

Spoon the potato mixture evenly over the kale. Sprinkle the rest of the cheese on top, then bake for 25 minutes or until the top is lightly browned. Allow your pie to rest for 15 minutes before serving so it can set slightly, and slice nicely.

SERVES SIX

Dutch Stampot

1 small onion, finely chopped

2 Tbsp (30 mL) vegetable oil

8 cups (2 L) kale leaves in chiffonade

¾ cup (180 mL) water

½ bouillon cube or equivalent

6 large floury potatoes, such as russets (about 3 lb/1.5 kg)

1 cup (250 mL) milk

4 Tbsp (60 mL) butter

Salt and black pepper

1 rookwurst or other large smoked sausage, cooked

*if using gluten-free sausage

Rookwurst—pronounced rokewurst—is a smoked sausage ring, traditionally served with stampot (literally, "stamped or mashed in a pot") in many Dutch households. Oma, my Dutch mother-in-law, bought her rookwurst at the horsemeat store on Hastings Street in Vancouver, BC, or at the Dutch store in New Westminster near the old Woodward's. The kale came from Holland via the Dutch store. It was in a large can labelled in Dutch with a picture of a kale leaf but it was almost puréed in consistency (and a little like baby food). We still loved the finished dish. Oma served her stampot with drippings kept in a special little pot in the fridge.

In a large skillet over medium heat, sauté the onions in the oil for a few minutes until softened. Add the kale and stir to coat with the onions and oil. Add the water and bouillon cube or equivalent. If you happen to have some stock, go ahead and use that. Continue to cook until kale is tender, about 10 minutes.

Meanwhile, boil the potatoes, drain and mash them with the milk and butter, adding salt and pepper to taste. The traditional way of serving stampot is to flatten the mashed potatoes on a warmed platter, make a shallow indentation for the kale, and place the sausage on top.

SERVES FOUR GENEROUSLY

"Modern" Stampot

1 lb (454 gr) turkey sausages

2 tsp (10 mL) vegetable oil

1 onion, finely chopped

3 cloves garlic, minced

2 cups (475 mL) canned tomatoes, chopped

6 cups (1.4 L) kale leaves, chopped

1 Tbsp (15 mL) balsamic vinegar

2 tsp (10 mL) Worcestershire sauce

½ cup (125 mL) water or stock (kale, vegetable or chicken)

2 lb (1 kg) 'Yukon Gold' potatoes (about 4) peeled, cut in chunks

½ cup (125 mL) milk, warmed

2 Tbsp (30 mL) butter

Black pepper

Parsley leaves for garnish

*if non-gluten Worcestershire sauce and sausage are used

Credit for this recipe goes to my neighbour Jackie, whose husband, Quincy, is Dutch. This is for sure more kid-friendly than the kind all the Omas made using that canned kale from Holland.

In a large skillet (with lid) big enough to eventually hold everything but the mashed potatoes, fry the sausages in the oil over medium heat until lightly browned and fully cooked. Remove from skillet and set aside. Drain most of the fat off, leaving a bit for the onions and garlic. Sauté the onions a few minutes over medium heat; add the garlic and continue to sauté until onions are softened, about 5 minutes.

Add the tomatoes, kale, balsamic vinegar and Worcestershire. Cover the skillet, then lower the heat and simmer, stirring occasionally. Add stock or water if mixture becomes too dry, cooking until kale is tender—about 10 minutes. Add the reserved sausages to the pan; cover and keep warm.

Boil the potatoes in salted water until tender, then drain and "stamp" (mash) with the milk, butter and pepper. Spoon the mashed potatoes onto a warmed platter, making an indentation or well in the centre. Fill the well with the kale and sausage mixture, and garnish with a little chopped parsley.

SERVES THREE TO FOUR

Gujerati Kale Bharta

8 cups (2 L) kale leaves, chopped

1 small rutabaga or turnip, peeled and cut in small dice

1 cup (250 mL) water

1 tsp (5 mL) salt

3 Tbsp (45 mL) butter or ghee for frying

1 onion, finely chopped

1 Tbsp (15 mL) ginger root or more, finely minced

1 tsp (5 mL) paprika or chili powder

½ tsp (2.5 mL) cumin seeds

¼ tsp (1 mL) cayenne

2 tsp (10 mL) garam masala

Juice of 1 lemon

About ½ cup (125 mL) cashews, lightly toasted and chopped, to garnish

Raita:

1 cup (250 mL) yogurt

8–10 mint leaves, stems removed, chopped very fine

1 green onion, minced

½ apple, chopped fine

Pinch of salt

Pinch of black pepper

½ tsp (2.5 mL) sugar

If you've never made Indian food before, don't be put off—it's easier than you think. You can even chop the veggies in the food processor if you like. This is delicious with brown or white basmati rice, chapatti and mint raita. Garnishing with a handful of lightly toasted cashews adds crunch and a complementary protein.

Simmer greens and turnip in a covered pan with 1 cup (250 mL) water and salt.

When tender, remove from heat and mash.

Heat ghee or butter in a skillet. Lightly fry the onion, ginger, paprika, cumin and cayenne for about 5 minutes or until cumin seeds pop. Add the mashed greens and stir-fry, adding a little water if necessary, until greens are well cooked. Just before serving, stir in the garam masala and lemon juice and sprinkle cashews on top. If you like, serve the kale bharta with raita.

For the raita: mix all ingredients well, and serve alongside the bharta.

SERVES FOUR

Eat-Your-Greens Meatloaf

2 pieces of sturdy bread, crusts removed, torn in small pieces

½ cup (125 mL) milk

½ tsp (2.5 mL) salt

4 cups (1 L) kale leaves in chiffonade

½ cup (125 mL) onion, chopped

1 lb (454 gr) lean ground beef

1 lb (454 gr) lean ground pork

1 large egg

2 tsp (10 mL) Dijon or grainy mustard

Salt and black pepper

½ tsp (2.5 mL) fresh thyme leaves, minced

1 tsp (5 mL) dried basil

½ tsp (2.5 mL) dried oregano

½ cup (125 mL) parsley leaves, minced

Optional Glaze:

½ cup (125 mL) ketchup

2 Tbsp (30 mL) brown sugar

1 Tbsp (15 mL) tamari or soy sauce

*if non-gluten bread, ketchup and soy sauce are used

This is a great meal for kids. Substitute ground turkey or bison for the beef and pork if you prefer, or use whatever combination of ground meat you like. You can use a food processor to chop the kale, then add in everything else, making this dish as quick as a wink to make. This meatloaf makes wonderful sandwiches for lunch, too, so hopefully you'll have leftovers!

Put the bread, milk and salt in a bowl that will eventually hold all the ingredients. Mix and let stand about 10 minutes until the bread soaks up the milk and mixture is soft.

Preheat oven to 350F (175C). Add the rest of the ingredients to the bread/milk mixture. Mix well, then pile evenly into a lightly greased casserole or large loaf pan. Bake for about 45 minutes. For the glaze, combine ingredients and brush or spoon evenly on top of the loaf after it has baked for 20 minutes.

SERVES SIX

Green Elizabeth

⅔ cup (160 mL) panko crumbs

⅔ cup (160 mL) flour

Salt and black pepper

1 tsp (5 mL) sugar (helps brown the crust)

3 Tbsp (45 mL) butter

1½ cups (350 mL) Emmental or Gruyère, grated, divided

1 lb (454 gr) waxy potatoes, halved and thinly sliced

3 medium leeks, trimmed and sliced thinly

8 cups (2 L) kale leaves and tender stems, chopped

1 large red bell pepper, diced

Pinch chili flakes

1 tart apple, peeled and chopped

1 cup (250 mL) sour cream, ricotta or mascarpone (optional)

What other people's mothers called apple crisp or cobbler, my mother called "Brown Betty." Apparently, it dates back to colonial times and has the distinction of having been Nancy Reagan's most requested dessert when she lived at the White House.

This is most decidedly a savoury version of "Brown Betty"; a huge frying pan or skillet makes steaming the veggies easy, and panko adds the crunch. The sour cream or ricotta makes it richer, if you are in the mood. Gewürztraminer is wonderful with this, and would set off the Emmental or Gruyère nicely.

Combine panko, flour, salt and pepper and sugar. Cut in butter with pastry blender, fingers or knives to make the crumble topping. Add ½ cup (125 mL) of the cheese. Set aside.

Preheat oven to 375F (190C) with oven rack in the middle position.

In a very large skillet or wide-bottomed pot, steam potatoes in a little salted water for about 4 minutes. Strew leeks on top, then the kale on top of leeks, then the bell and chili flakes and apple. Ensure there's enough water still in the pan, then with the lid on, steam 5 minutes or until veggies are wilted. Drain, and—yes, I'm going to say it again—save the yummy liquid for soup.

Pile veggies into a large buttered baking dish, smoothing the surface.

Add the sour cream, ricotta or mascarpone if you're using it to top the veggies. Use the back of a spoon to smear and level. Strew remaining cheese on top. Cover with topping, patting lightly to cover the surface evenly.

Bake about 25 minutes until Betty is bubbly and the top golden brown.

Serve with a big salad and crusty, dense bread.

SERVES FOUR GENEROUSLY

Endnotes

1. R. Jacobs, Jr, Ella H. Haddad, Amy Joy Lanou and Mark J. Messina, "Food, Plant Food, and Vegetarian Diets in the U.S. Dietary Guidelines: Conclusions of an Expert Panel," in "Fifth International Congress on Vegetarian Nutrition," supplement, *American Journal of Clinical Nutrition* 89 (2009): S1549–S1552.

2. Gerald F. Combs, Jr., "Vitamin K," in *The Vitamins: Fundamental Aspects in Nutrition and Health*, 2nd ed. (San Diego: Academic Press, 1998), 225–44.

3. Talwinder Singh Kahlon, Mei-Chen Chiu and Mary H. Chapman, "Steam Cooking Significantly Improves in Vitro Bile Acid Binding of Collard Greens, Kale, Mustard Greens, Broccoli, Green Bell Pepper, and Cabbage," *Nutrition Research* 28, no. 6 (2008): 351–57

4. Young Jin Moon, Xiaodong Wang, Marilyn E. Morris, "Dietary Flavonoids: Effects on Xenobiotic and Carcinogen Metabolism," *Toxicology in Vitro* 20, no. 2 (2006): 187–210.

5. Ibid.

6. Dean A. Kopsell and David E. Kopsell, "Carotenoids in Vegetables: Biosynthesis, Occurrence, Impacts on Human Health, and Potential for Manipulation," in *Bioactive Foods in Promoting Health: Fruits and Vegetables*, ed. Ronald Ross Watson and Victor R. Preedy (San Diego: Academic Press, 2010), 645–62.

7. "Raw Foods," Lutein Information Bureau, accessed December 2011, http://www.luteininfo.com/whereraw.

8. Dean A. Kopsell and David E. Kopsell, "Carotenoids in Vegetables: Biosynthesis, Occurrence, Impacts on Human Health, and Potential for Manipulation," in *Bioactive Foods in Promoting Health: Fruits and Vegetables*, ed. Ronald Ross Watson and Victor R. Preedy (San Diego: Academic Press, 2010), 645–62.

9. Elizabeth H. Jeffery and Marcela Araya, "Physiological Effects of Broccoli Consumption," *Phytochemical Reviews* 8, no. 1 (2009): 283–98.

10. Mario G. Ferruzzi and Joshua Blakeslee, "Digestion, Absorption, and Cancer Preventative Activity of Dietary Chlorophyll Derivatives," *Nutrition Research* 27, no. 1 (2007): 1–12.

11. G.S. Stoewsand, "Bioactive Organosulfur Phytochemicals in *Brassica oleracea* Vegetables—A Review," *Food and Chemical Toxicology* 33, no. 6 (1995): 537–43.

12. "Health & Horticultural Research at UNH: Leafy Greens at the Leading Edge," Peg Boyles, University of New Hampshire Cooperative Extension, posted March 10, 2006, http://extension.unh.edu/news/2006/03/health_horticultural_research.html

13. Dean A. Kopsell, David E. Kopsell, Mark G. Lefsrud, Joanne Curran–Celentano and Laura E. Dukach, "Variation in Lutein, B–carotene, and Chlorophyll Concentrations Among *Brassica oleraceae* Cultigens and Seasons," *HortScience* 39, no. 2 (2004): 361–64.

Index

Seed Sources

CANADA AND THE UNITED STATES

Baker Creek Heirloom Seeds
This company has a catalogue that is worth ordering. They proffer 'Ragged Jack' (a.k.a. 'Red Russian'), 'Dwarf Siberian' and 'Blue-Curled Scotch'. If you are a sweet-pea fan, check out their varieties—they have lots, and the seeds are generously packed.

Fedco
With several varieties of kale on offer, this co-op seed company has introduced 'Beedy's Camden Kale'—which has reportedly survived well at temperatures as low as -20F (-29C), nothing to sneeze at.

Johnny's Selected Seeds
Johnny's is an employee-owned seed company and you won't be bored with 'Ripbor' (organic), 'Starbor' and 'Winterbor'. All are F1 hybrids so growth is uniform, but seeds saved won't produce a copy of the same plant—they either revert to one or the other parent-type kale, or are sterile. Johnny's carries many types of seed for microgreens as well.

Renee's Garden Seeds
Renee Shepherd was the first to introduce the 'Lacinato' (Tuscan) variety of kale to North America in the 1980s. With pretty water-coloured seed packages and fair pricing, Renee's seeds are available online or in garden centres in Canada and the U.S. In 2012, the Portuguese kale known as 'Tronchuda Beira' is their new offering.

Salt Spring Seeds
Located on Salt Spring Island in BC, Dan Jason grows his own organic seed. Look for 'Laurel's Frilly Kale', from *Laurel's Kitchen* cookbook fame.

Territorial Seed Company
This Oregon company offers seed in small/medium/large and larger quantities, and proffers many varieties of kale including 'Red Chidori', 'Fizz', and 'White Russian'.

West Coast Seeds
This seed retailer's offerings for 2012 include 'Winterbor' F1 (super curly!) 'Vates Blue-Curled Scots', 'Redbor' F1, and the beautiful, various-hued 'Rainbow Tuscan'. Offers different sized packages, too.

Wild Garden Seeds
Frank Morton's breeding work with kale and other veggies is legendary. Offerings include 'Lacinato Rainbow' (a.k.a. 'Rainbow Tuscan'; lasts very long in the garden), 'Old Growth Palm' (for your dinosaur or walking-stick garden), 'Red Ruffled', 'Wild Garden Kales' (try these in your kale forest), 'White Russian', 'Red Ursa', 'Wild Red' and 'Winter Red'. Check out their Insectary Mix, which provides a year-around source of food "your resident beneficials can count on."

UNITED KINGDOM
Please note: sometimes you will find kale listed as "borecole."

D.T. Brown
A good selection of kale including 'Walking Stick' and 'Darkibor' F1.

Dobies
'Red Russian', 'Nero di Toscano', and 'Green Curled Afro'.

Edwin Tucker & Sons
'Darkibor' F1, 'Hungry Gap' (because it "bridged the gap" when there were little other vegetables in the garden), 'Ripbor' F1 and 'Fizz'—pretty, small and uniform.

Kings Seeds
Beautiful, low-growing 'Scarlet' and 'Dwarf Green Curled'.

Real Seeds
'Sutherland', "Càil Cataibh" in Gaelic, "shrugged off attack by aphids, cabbage white caterpillars, ravenous goats, and 70 mph freezing sleet overwinter"! Also offering 'East Friesian Palm', 'True Siberian', and 'Red Ursa'.

Suffolk Seeds
Look for 'Westlandse Winter' and 'Thousandhead' English heirloom kale.

Unwins
'Dwarf Winnetou' and 'Kapitan', new to me, both curly varieties.

FRANCE

Graines Baumaux
Chou 'Jagalo Nero', 'Halbhoher Gruner Krause', Chou frisee 'Reflex' F1 et 'Frostara'.